Essential
Mexico

by
PETER McGREGOR EADIE

PASSPORT BOOKS
a division of *NTC Publishing Group*
Lincolnwood, Illinois USA

Published by Passport Books, a division of NTC Publishing Group, 4255 West Touhy Avenue, Lincolnwood (Chicago), Illinois 60646–1975 U.S.A.

Copyright © 1994 by the Automobile Association

The contents of this publication are believed correct at the time of printing. Nevertheless, the publishers cannot accept responsibility for errors or omissions, nor for changes in details given. We are always grateful to readers who let us know of any errors or omissions they come across, and future printings will be updated accordingly.

Published by Passport Books in conjunction with The Automobile Association of Great Britain.

Written by Peter McGregor Eadie
"Peace and Quiet" section by Paul Sterry

Library of Congress Catalog
Card Number 93–85600
ISBN 0–8442–8922–1

10 9 8 7 6 5 4 3 2 1

PRINTED IN TRENTO, ITALY

Front cover picture: Mexican fishermen

The weather chart displayed on **page 108** of this book is calibrated in °C and millimetres. For conversion to °F and inches simply use the following formula:

$$25 \cdot 4mm = 1 \text{ inch} \qquad °F = 1 \cdot 8 \times °C + 32$$

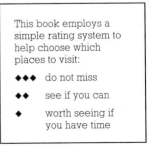

This book employs a
simple rating system to
help choose which
places to visit:

◆◆◆   do not miss

◆◆   see if you can

◆   worth seeing if
        you have time

INTRODUCTION

Mexico has been a favourite holiday venue of Americans for many years and is now becoming a popular, long-haul destination for Europeans. This special country offers a magnificent range of scenery, and many fascinating places to visit.

The borders of Mexico have changed many times in the course of her history. They could be said to extend further south during Mesoamerican times, when the Mayas were rulers of all of the foot of Central America, and the untamed Indian tribes of the north lived beyond the central plateau. After the Spanish conquered Mexico and made it part of their empire, Mexico extended considerably north of her present border to include parts of California, Arizona and Texas.

Today, Mexico is four times the size of Spain, bordered in the north by the Rio Grande, which threads its way from Brownsville to El Paso; but no natural line of demarcation separates it from California, Arizona and New Mexico, which are now part of the USA. In the south, the border runs along the northern edge of Guatemala and Belice, cutting off the heel of the southern part of Central America. The rest of the foot now belongs to several other Central American states. To the west lies the Pacific Ocean and the Gulf of California, and the eastern border is created by the Gulf of Mexico and the Caribbean, giving Mexico thousands of miles of coastline, varying from sandy beaches to rugged cliffs. Mexico has hot desert in the north, fertile plateaux, mainly around the centre, and jungle lowlands. Two-thirds of the country are encrusted with mountains, some of which are always covered with snow. Altogether, 22 peaks tower over 10,000 feet (3,048m) above sea level. The highest lies close to Veracruz, where Hernán Cortés, the Spanish Conquistador, first landed. It is called the Pico de Orizaba and is 18,855 feet (5,747m) high. Two mountain ranges stretch southward from Mexico's northern border: the Sierra Madre Occidental and the Sierra Madre

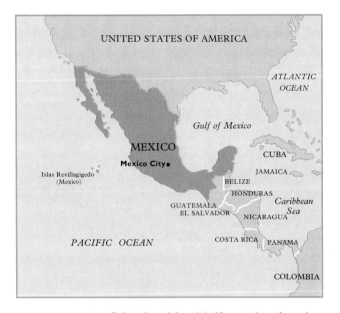

Oriental, and they join like a string of pearls south of Mexico City. Geological pressures have also created several mountain ranges around Oaxaca, which fall away at the narrow isthmus of Tehuantepec on the southeast. Volcanoes are plentiful in Mexico. The last major volcanic eruption took place some 45 years ago. A farmworker saw some smoke rising from a fissure and tried to smother it with soil, but was unable to do so because, after a small series of explosions, the ground opened up before him. Next day, enough ash had accumulated to create a 100-foot (30m) mound. Today this mound has grown into a volcano called Paricutín. It lies to the west of Mexico City and stands 3,000 feet (914m) high, with a crater which is 1,000 feet (309m) across.

Although there are many mountains in Mexico, rivers and lakes are few. The largest lake lies near Guadalajara, and is called Lake Chapala; two smaller but very attractive lakes are Pátzcuaro and Cuitzeo in Michoacán. It is worth touring these lakes by

INTRODUCTION

A gigantic statue of José Morelos, a Mexican hero, dominates the tiny island of Janítzio on Lake Pátzcuaro

speedboat if you are in the vicinity. Río Balsas is the longest river; rising in the state of Tlaxcala and flowing into the Pacific Ocean, it is only navigable for short lengths.

Something for everyone

Most people who visit Mexico follow one of three kinds of activity: visiting archaeological sites, of which there is an abundance, much on the same scale of magnitude as Egypt; visiting colonial towns, many of which abound with palaces, churches and cathedrals built during the days when Mexico was part of the great Spanish empire; and visiting magnificent beach resorts, bordering both the Pacific and the Caribbean.

When Hernán Cortés arrived in 1519 at the huge causeways of Tenochtitlán (the Mexico City of the Aztecs), there was no one to tell him that he had come upon one of the richest cultural countries in the New World; a country which could match any other in architectural magnificence, with over 11,000 archaeological sites.

Some 470 years later, much has changed, and visitors can take a classical tour to many sites and see for themselves. These tours usually begin in Mexico City, which was the former Aztec capital. Next stop is Oaxaca, to see the

Zapotec and Mixtec sites of Monte Albán, Yagul and Mitla, and then on to Villahermosa to see the Olmec influences at La Venta Park, which started it all. The final stop is then Yucatán peninsula, which is studded with city states from the Mayan civilisation, whose inhabitants had a knowledge of mathematics and astronomy, far in advance of Europe at that time. An accurate calendar of 365 days had been worked out and their system of numbers was far superior to that of the Romans, which served our world for centuries. Site stops include Palenque, Uxmal and Chichén Itzá, all built on the grand scale. These classical tours provide the visitor with a startling insight into the great civilisations that developed in Mesoamerica prior to the arrival of the Europeans. To obtain the maximum benefit, it is advisable to visit the National Museum of Archaeology in Mexico City, which gives an excellent historical background to the development of these times.

Colonial Architecture
The period of New Spain lasted 300 years, from the victory of the Conquistadores in 1521 until Independence, and colonial architectural tours examine the influences and styles of this era. History offers no more rewarding field of exploration than the study of the interaction of two great civilisations, Mesoamerican Indian and Catholic Spanish, totally unacquainted with each other. The visitor interested in Colonial Mexico will see some of the finest stately homes, palaces, churches and cathedrals anywhere in the world, which arose from the contribution each culture gave to the other.

Beach Resorts
As one would expect from a country that is edged with 6,212 miles (9,995km) of golden sand, Mexico has very sophisticated resort cities, including the famous Acapulco on the Pacific side and Cancún in the Caribbean. Developments are taking place continually, and among the new places to look out for is Huatulco, which, besides having several smart hotels, now has a splendid Club Med.

The resorts of Baja California are paradise for fishermen, surfers and swimmers

Off the West Coast and hanging like a pendant is the peninsula of Baja California, separated from the mainland by the Gulf of California. Along the shoreline here are resorts which offer some of the best fishing anywhere in the world. Ensenada is known as the 'Yellowtail Capital of the World' and the locals claim in Cabo San Lucas and San José del Cabo that 40,000 marlin are caught every year in water off the capes.

From the coastal towns of Los Mochis, on the mainland side of the Gulf of California, to Chihuahua runs one of the world's most scenic railway routes. It takes 12 hours and passes through the Copper Canyon, which is larger and higher than the Grand Canyon in the USA.

The exceptional coastline has more than enough room to accommodate a variety of holiday resorts, ranging from quiet venues that were once fishing villages to Cancún, which attracts a million visitors a year with its high life and sizzling entertainment.

BACKGROUND

Origins

The earliest trace of *homo sapiens* found in Mexico was uncovered some 20 years ago during road construction developments near the archaeological site of Tipacoya. Radio-carbon dating indicates that these remains are 20,000 years old.

In most parts of the continent to the north of Mesoamerica the early economy was based on hunting and gathering. Only at a comparatively later date than in Mesoamerica did agricultural development take place in certain regions of North America, whereas in Mexico explorations over a wide area, stretching from Chiapas to Tamanlipas, have established that early species of wild maize corn were intensively gathered and eventually cultivated. Research shows that the evolution of wild corn to full cultivation took place between 8,000BC and 1,000BC. Such agricultural development would have been essential to the creation of the early city states of Mesoamerica.

Before the Spaniards arrived, and when there were no cities in North America, it is estimated that there were up to 20 million Indians living in Mexico. These figures reflect the high level of civilisation which existed in Mesoamerica in Pre-Columbian times. The Europeans decimated these numbers by bringing with them diseases against which the Indians had no resistance, and by cruelly overworking the Indians in near starvation conditions. By the 17th century the pure-blooded Indians who provided the main labour force had dwindled from some nine million on the Mexican central plateau to two and a half million.

Following the conquest, Mexico's population was divided into a caste system as well defined as that found among the Hindus. At the top of the pile were the *gachupines*, who were Spaniards born in Spain. They had control of both spiritual and political life and all government officials belonged to this group. Next came the Creoles who, although born in Mexico, were pure-blooded

Spaniards. They were denied government office but many were wealthy, thanks to the exploitation of cheap labour from the Indians who worked their *encomiendas* or mines. The third category were the *mestizos*, who were of mixed Spanish and Indian blood. Unlike the

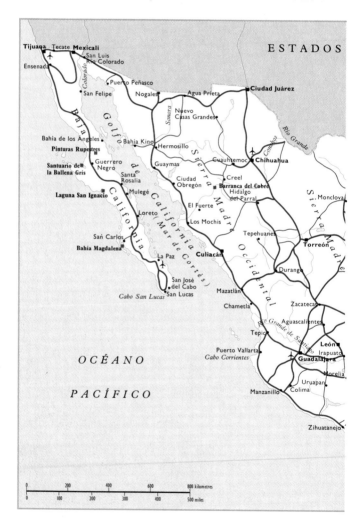

English and Dutch settlers who came to live on the eastern seaboard of North America, the Spaniards brought very few European women with them; hence, unions were formed with Indian women. One of the astonishing facts about New Spain is the small number of

Europeans who came to live in Mexico during the first three centuries following the conquest. A census taken in 1793 showed that only 8,000 Europeans were spread throughout the whole country.

Today the population of Mexico is in the region of 80 million people, with 20 million citizens living and working in Mexico City, making it the largest metropolis in the world. Big efforts are being made by the government through employment schemes to spread the population more evenly. But at present about 2,000 people move to Mexico City each day to seek employment.

Olmecs

The Olmec civilisation is popularly considered the mother culture, and her heartland spread over 11,350 square miles (29,396 sq km) on the shores of the Caribbean, now mainly the jungles of southern Veracruz and Tabasco. Today, the antiquities of the Olmec civilisation are more likely to be found in museums than on original sites. The Olmecs venerated the Jaguar as supernatural and many of their artefacts found throughout Mexico feature human beings with the snub nose of a cat and fangs.

Three main archaeological sites have been discovered within the Olmec heartland: San Lorenzo, with its remarkably advanced system of drainage; La Venta, where there is now a park in which the visitor can see several colossal heads which are 10 feet (3m) high and weigh up to 20 tons/tonnes. Stone sculpture is the supreme hallmark of Olmec art and in the park can also be seen caparisoned figure reliefs, stelae and rock carvings; and Tres Zapotes, which came into being after La Venta, around 500BC, and went on until 100BC, and which stretches along the bank of the Hueypan River.

Teotihuacános

After a long process of development, the Mesoamerican inhabitants of the Valley of Mexico founded the city of Teotihuacán, some 30 miles (48km) northeast of the present capital. Greater than contemporary Imperial Rome, the city was probably the finest ever

In Teotihuacán, the sacred city of Quetzalcoatl, the Avenue of the Dead ends at the Pyramid of the Moon

built in Mexico. It covered an area of 14 square miles (36.26 sq km) and at its height had a population of over 200,000 people. Development in Teotihuacán (the name means 'the place where men become gods') spans a period of nearly 900 years, beginning around 100BC and ending around AD750. The grandeur of the site is seen to lie along a broad thoroughfare known as the 'Avenue of the Dead'. Along this most sacred artery is a series of stone platforms known as *talud-tableros*. When the city was inhabited these formed a stone frame for magnificent murals, and were a constant reminder that this was a city of the gods. At the heart of the city is the giant Pyramid of the Sun, rising to a height of 200 feet (61m).

At the other end, the *Ciudadela* is dominated by a splendid six-tiered temple dedicated to Quetzalcoatl – the serpent god, and Tlaloc – the rain god. Both are of supreme importance in Mexican mythology. During its long history, Teotihuacán extended its influence through the valleys of Mexico, Puebla, Tlaxcala and Morelos, and stretched as far as Chametla near the coastal town of Mazatlán, some 900 miles (1,440km) distant. Penetration along the Gulf was equally strong, reaching from Cerro de las Messos in the south to Huexteca in the north. Traces of her culture have also been found in the northwest.

Toltecs

When the Teotihuacános finally abandoned their city, new groups from the north descended on to the Central Plateau. As time passed, these tribes converged and became known as the Toltecs. Their capital became Tula, an archaeological site 50 miles (80km) north of Mexico City in the state of Hidalgo. This is considered to be the legendary Tollan from which the Toltec culture dominated Mesoamerica from AD859 to 1250. After the demise of Teotihuacán, other cities such as Xochicalco, Cholula and Cacaxtla grew in importance.

Of primary interest in Tula is the Temple of Tlahuizcalpantecuhtli, dedicated to the morning star – Quetzalcoatl – in one of his manifestations. On the platform stand giant warrior sculptures 16 feet (4.8m) high. They look out over the surrounding landscape from a height of 6,700 feet (2,042m) as though remembering back a thousand years to their once great civilisation. They originally supported the wooden roof of the temple, which has long since disappeared. On the chest of each warrior is a stylised butterfly, the Toltec emblem.

In the mythology of the Mesoamerican civilisations of the Central Plateau, Quetzalcoatl was the bearded god of learning and priesthood and during the Toltec period there arose a great priest, whose name was Ce Acatl Topilzin, and who founded the city of Tula. Because of his deep wisdom he began to be called Quetzalcoatl, and for the first time this name became linked with a man of ideas and spiritual development. His reign is remembered as one of peace and plenty. Legend told that he would return in the future and when Hernán Cortés landed in Mexico the Aztecs thought at first that he was Quetzalcoatl returning, which created terror

The gigantic columns on the Pyramid of the Morning Star at Tula are masterpieces of Toltec sculpture

in the hearts of their leaders.

The ceremonial centre of this ancient city contains a ball-court and the remains of other interesting constructions, including flagstone avenues, colonnades, and *talud-tableros*.

Totonacs

The Totonac civilisation reached its peak between AD700 and 1100, and El Tajín is its most famous city. Set in the densely-forested regions in the state of Veracruz, these splendid ruins include the impressive Pyramid of Niches, whose 365 niches represent the days of the year.

An important ceremony, to which the Totonacs subscribed, was the dance of El Volador, which was performed as a religious rite. It is most impressive and can still be seen as a folklore spectacle, particularly in nearby Papantla. It used to take place only on the feast of Corpus Christi, but can nowadays be seen on most Sundays in the main square. Five performers climb to the top of a very high pole, which has four extended arms like a cross at the top. One performer stands at the top on a small platform in the centre, where he dances and plays haunting music on his pipe, and occasionally beats a small drum attached to his waistband, while the others, dressed to represent the colourful plumage of the macaw, the symbol of the sun, secure themselves by the ankle with ropes and leap off into space, with arms extended. All four fly round the pole exactly 13 times. The four encirclements of 13 makes up the mystical figure of 52, to represent the 52-year cycle of ancient Mesoamerica.

The Zapotecs and Mixtecs

The ruins of the sacred city of the Zapotecs lies just outside the beautiful colonial town of Oaxaca. It is called Monte Albán, meaning 'White Mountain'. To build this city the Zapotecs had to level the summit, construct retaining walls and lay out terraces. On top of the mountain are long rows of tombs in parallel lines flanking the plaza. Many elaborate tombs have been found stocked with funerary urns, which portray their different gods. They were also filled with precious stones and the walls were painted

The magnificent Gran Plaza of Monte Albán is built on a levelled mountain top

with frescoes.

The first traces of civilisation in the Monte Albán area are thought to go back 1,000 years before Christ. It is interesting to note that although the Zapotecs lived in this region for centuries, the height of their civilisation corresponds with the classical age of Teotihuacán. Cultural influences were received from outside their domain, but because of their geographical isolation the Zapotecs naturally developed their own distinctive style of architecture.

By about AD900, the Zapotecs began departing from the city and rival Zapotec cities in the Oaxaca Valley began to assume authority. The ruins of the two most important of these, Yagul and Mitla, are easily reached by car in a couple of hours' drive from Oaxaca.

The Mixtecs came through the Coixtláhuaca Pass into the Oaxaca Valley some time after the Zapotecs. They took over Monte Albán and revitalised it in their own style. The Mixtecs' claim to fame lay in their fine craftsmanship in precious metals, and their skill in the field of ceramics, with their potteries producing delicate vessels decorated with geometric motifs, glyphs and images of their gods. They also excelled in the production of turquoise mosaics. Mixtec history is well recorded in codices made from strips of deer skin joined together, often to a length of 25 feet (10.6m). On them were beautiful explanatory paintings of important events. These skins were usually folded like screens and stored as books.

When the new tribe of Aztecs entered Mexico from the north and overran central Mexico, the Mixtecs frequently found themselves conquered in battle and having to pay tributes to Tenochtitlán. Both the Zapotecs and the Mixtecs survived these hardships and those put upon them by the Spaniards, and today their descendants can be seen dressed in striking Indian attire going about their daily lives in Oaxaca.

The Maya

The Maya were the largest homogenous

BACKGROUND

group of Indians north of Peru, and their cultural development began around 1500BC and spread over an area of 250,000 square miles (650,000 sq km). The geographical scope of their civilisation is divided into three major regions.

The southern region comprises the Guatemalan Highlands, part of Chiapas, Pacific coastal Guatemala and a section of El Salvador. The central region, sometimes referred to as the southern lowlands, includes the Peten of Guatemala, the Usumacinata River drainage into Tabasco, Belice, the Montagua River of Guatemala, southern Campeche and westernmost Honduras. The northern region, sometimes referred to as the northern lowlands, contains the rest of the Yucatán peninsula, with the magnificent site of Chichén Itzá, which is only one of many great cities pertaining to this amazing civilisation.

Many of the Maya cities, still in an interesting state of preservation, are designed along similar lines as other Mesoamerican cities. At the centre of the city were the main temples and spacious plaza. These were the places where important religious and anniversary rituals and events were celebrated. Close to this area were the homes of the priests and the lords and officials who were responsible for government and administration. Further out were the houses of the rich and important merchants, and on the perimeter were the dwellings of ordinary citizens, including the farmers, who worked the land surrounding the city and supplied the food for the populace. Maya cities were always situated close to natural water-holes called *cenotes*, which were essential to survival in this hot climate.

The Maya's knowledge of astronomy and mathematics was immense. Some of their calculations have proved not only to be well in advance of their time but more accurate than those that we use today. They include a more exact calendar than the one we use today and the working out of the lunar cycles, and the accurate prediction of eclipses.

The advanced knowledge of astronomy and

From the top of El Castillo, or the Pyramid of Kukulkan, is a view over the Mayan city of Chichén Itzá

mathematics is mostly credited to the Maya civilisation, but it became, or was, fundamental knowledge comprehended by all the main Mesoamerican civilisations. There was considerable intercommunication between the various co-existing city states and they traded extensively among themselves. Trade routes stretched from Yucatán to the northeast of Mexico and as far south as Panama, and cocoa beans were the main form of coinage.

The Aztecs

In the chronology of Mesoamerican Indian civilisations, the Aztecs arrived late. They came down from Aztlán (Place of Herons) in the Mexican Highlands in the early 13th century. During their migration they acquired the name Mexica.

After wandering the marshes in the region of the Mexico Valley, they came across an eagle perched on a cactus devouring a snake. This fulfilled an ancient tribal prophesy, and here they knew they must settle and build their home. This they did and Tenochtitlán became the home of the Aztec or Mexican people. The eagle devouring the serpent remains to this day the heraldic

BACKGROUND

symbol at the centre of the Mexican flag. The capital grew into one of the greatest cities the world has ever seen, according to the Spanish conquistadores. It housed a population of a quarter of a million people and was laid out with a great criss-cross of canals. A model of it can be seen in the Museo Nacional de Antropoligía (Museum of Anthropology) in Mexico City.

Magnificent causeways, capable of carrying 20 soldiers abreast, linked the capital on Lake Texcoco to the mainland on three sides. The centre of the city, close to where the main cathedral stands today, was a giant pyramid, with its twin temples dedicated to Tlaloc the rain god and Huitzilpochtli the sun god. Surrounding this great capital, were farmlands that provided the produce which fed the city populace and enabled Tenochtitlán to become the ecclesiastical, civil and military centre of a great empire. In their effort to eradicate all other religious beliefs, the Spaniards unfortunately did a very thorough job of destroying and dismantling Tenochtitlán, even to the point of filling in the canals and much of the lake upon which it was built.

Although little remains of Tenochtitlán, there are some minor remains of Tenayuca in the suburbs of Mexico City, and some smaller Aztec pyramids at Santa Cecilia and Calixtlahuaca. Well worthwhile is a visit to Malinalco, dramatically set in the mountains some 30 miles (48km) from Toluca. Here you will see a temple dedicated to two great military orders of the Aztecs, the Knights of the Jaguar and the Knights of the Eagle. Aztec sculpture has fared better than architecture, and two particularly fine monumental works excavated in the 18th century can now be seen in Hall 7 in the Museo Nacional de Antropoligía.

Great as the Aztec civilisation was, its role in the history of the New World was similar to that of Ancient Rome to Greece. Although it continued to improve building and engineering skills, it also marked the onset of decadence and a move away from original religious thought.

The Spanish Conquest

In the latter part of the 15th century Christopher Columbus, on an expedition funded by the Spanish Crown, discovered the island of Cuba, which lies off the east coast of Mexico. Cuba became the base from which Hernán Cortés set sail for Mesoamerica in 1519.

Cortés landed in Veracruz, whence legend said Quetzalcoatl sailed a few centuries earlier, promising to return. Cortés, who also had a fair skin and beard, actually arrived in the year prophesied for the god's return. The scouts of Moctezuma, leader of the Aztecs, reported that Cortés had embarked from a 'floating mountain', which also heightened the atmosphere of fear and awe. The arrival of horses which were unknown to the Indians and thought to be four-legged creatures with men issuing from their backs, and the Spaniards' ability to kill from afar using muskets, strengthened the belief that Cortés was a god.

Destroyed by the Spanish, little remains of the glories of the great Aztec cities

These are some of the ingredients which led,

against unbelievable odds, to a few Spanish adventurers conquering a vast empire. Within two years of landing, Cortés was to bring about the surrender of the Aztecs. Before leaving for his trek through the interior to the capital of Mexico, Cortés ordered the ships in which his party arrived to be burnt, so that there could be no retreat. This act did much to concentrate the minds of his soldiers to the task in hand, for it was now a case of conquer or die.

Cortés was extremely skilful at winning over people to his cause, thus increasing the size of his army. In this, he was considerably helped by the behaviour of the Aztecs, who were continually demanding heavy tributes and men for sacrifice from outlying tribes. Considerable resentment against the centralised rule of Tenochtitlán had already built up. Those tribes who were opposed to the conquistador's ambitions were savagely massacred.

Cortés marched his army over the high Sierras to conquer the Aztec capital, Tenochtitlán

When Cortés had completed his long march, climbing the high pass between the mountains of Popocatépetl and Iztaccíhuatl, Moctezuma came out along the southern causeway to

welcome him. The Spaniards were treated with great hospitality. They were housed as honoured guests in the palace of Axayacatl, the former home of Moctezuma's father. Now, in a daring stroke, Cortés took Moctezuma captive and changed a potentially dangerous situation in which he could have been ambushed to one of being in control. Cortés had to return to Veracruz and during his absence some of his Spanish troops in Tenochtitlán slaughtered many Aztec nobles while they were performing a ritual dance to their gods. The Aztecs, incensed at this affront, waited until Cortés returned before launching a savage attack. Cortés was severely routed, but he rounded up huge numbers of new Indian recruits and returned to the fray. In the battle which ensued the defenders of Tenochtitlán stood little chance. After a courageous defence, under the new Aztec leader, Cuauhtémoc, the capital fell to the Spaniards. The demise of the great Indian nation had begun.

It is interesting to note nowadays where Mexican sympathies lie in all this bloodbath of wars. Today there are no statues to Cortés, and the revival of interest in those times is mainly due to attempts to re-understand the great Mesoamerica Indian civilisations that existed prior to the founding of New Spain.

Colonial Mexico

Following the construction of the capital of New Spain on the ruins of the old Aztec capital, the country was now divided into huge estates or *encomiendas* under some 500 Spanish landlords. In return for 'looking after' the conquered Indians by educating them in European ways and converting them to the Catholic faith, the estate owners were entitled to their unpaid labour. This privilege was soon exploited and could be said to be a strong contributing factor to the later overthrow of colonialism.

In 1535, Antonio de Mendoza was appointed the first of 61 viceroys who were to rule Mexico for the next three centuries. He was a practical man, whose portrait can be seen in the Gallery of Viceroys in Chapultepec

Castle. His rule, and that of Cortés, saw the expansion of New Spain as far south as Honduras, as far north as Kansas and as far east as New Orleans.

As a result of their expansion, the Spanish were able to develop the mineral resources, particularly of silver and gold, of this enormously rich territory. With this wealth they built many beautiful cities with magnificent cathedrals and fine mansions. When the Aztecs were conquered, the Mesoamerican stonemasons could no longer practise their art in the building of pyramids and temples. However, Spanish architects soon employed their talents in the building of early colonial churches. Much of the beauty of these graceful edifices is due to the skill and imagination of the Nahuas, who responded enthusiastically to the opportunity. The intricate roof decorations of Santa Maria Tonantzintla, which is close to Puebla, often referred to as the Rome of America because of its numerous churches, is a fine example. Decorated with polychrome and gold leaf and thickly adorned with angels, strange little animals, mysterious flowers and gorgeous fruit, it is a wonder to behold.

By the beginning of the 19th century, Mexico was the richest of all the overseas territories belonging to Spain, but as a colony she had become an anachronism. She was quite capable of self-government. Indian exploitation, resentment by the Creoles who were still not allowed to hold high office but were extremely wealthy from land ownership and mining, and the heavy taxation and export controls levied by the Spanish Crown, contributed to national unrest. Add to these ingredients other contemporary influences, with the breakaway of the 13 American colonies from Britain and the French Revolution, and we see that the time was becoming ripe for change. All these circumstances led to the establishment of independence.

Independence
The Mexican War of Independence can be said to have begun when the Spanish

Now a national monument, San Miguel de Allende was home to Independence leader, Ignacio de Allende

government discovered a revolutionary plot. This caused a parish priest Miguel Hidalgo, now considered father of the revolution, to ring his parish bell summoning his villagers to arms. Soon 50,000 Mexicans rallied to Hidalgo's call, but the priest did not turn out to be as good a soldier as he was a revolutionary, and instead of allowing his authority to come under the control of Ignacio Allende, a soldier, Hidalgo lead the battle strategy, with disastrous consequences. Finally, Hidalgo and Allende were betrayed and captured, and later executed for treason in Chihuahua.

However, by this time the torch of independence had caught alight and the final struggle began in 1820, when an outstanding officer, Agustín de Iturbide took over and finally established independence. Iturbide declared himself Agustín I, Emperor of Mexico; but pride came before the fall and soon afterwards he lost the support of the militia and was banished.

In 1822, the new republic came into being. The Monumento a la Independencia (Monument of National Independence) stands as tall as a lighthouse on the Paseo de la Reforma in Mexico City, and if you cross the road to the island on which it stands you can see statues of the most outstanding heroes who were involved in the lengthy struggle. During the early decades of the Republic, the government was badly served by its leaders. There was no firm policy and precious little continuity, as one leader after another was removed from power by unconstitutional methods. From the establishment of Independence until the Revolution in 1910, Mexico had 40 presidents and two emperors. In 1846, the United States declared war on Mexico, and Santa Anna, the general whose army won victory at the battle of the Alamo, was forced to cede about half of Mexico's territory, including California, Arizona and New Mexico, to the United States.

Soon afterwards, Mexico elected her first genuine statesman, a Zapotec called Benito Juárez, as her president. Today his statue can be seen in nearly every city throughout the country. When he took over his bankrupt country, he was forced to suspend payment on foreign debts, which led to problems with France, Britain and Spain. French troops invaded Mexico and put Archduke Maximilian on the throne as the new emperor. Benito Juárez fought for the survival of an independent Mexico for the next three years against Maximilian and the French. Then Napoleon III recalled his troops, leaving Maximilian to be captured by the Mexican army, and shot. Juárez was able to reduce the national debt, restore Mexican industry and commerce, bring about agricultural reform and improve human rights and education. A few years after Juárez died, Porfirio Díaz came to power and undid much of the good which Juárez had established. Without regard for human rights or democracy, he established a secret police force and re-instituted the *haciendas* at the expense of the Indians, now the poorest members of the population. Díaz ruled for 35 years before the Mexican Revolution succeeded in ousting him in 1911.

From Revolution to the Present Day

Many prominent figures and heroes emerged

during the Revolution, of which the best known were Emiliano Zapata and 'Pancho' Villa. After several years of turbulence, stability was restored, with a new constitution being drawn up in 1917 at Querétaro. Politically, Mexico is now a well-established democracy, but for the last few decades there has been one ruling party, the Partido Revolucionario Institucional (PRI).

Recent years have seen progress in public welfare, including greater Social Security, the establishment of more schools and higher educational institutions, and an improvement in preventive medicine and health treatment. The mineral wealth of Mexico is enormous and the discovery of oil deposits in the Gulf has created a boom. Unfortunately, a decline in petroleum prices led to Mexico's foreign debts rising steeply. But the new President, Carlos Salinas de Gortari, who was elected in 1988, has taken giant strides to resolve the rising inflation created by this problem. At the same time the Mexican Ministry of Tourism has worked hard to improve the tourism industry which is bringing in hard currency from abroad, creating enormous interest in their country, and attracting visitors from near and far.

Brightly painted boats carry visitors around the Floating Gardens of Xochimilco

MEXICO CITY AND ITS ENVIRONS

Mexico City, the nation's capital, is located in the country's central highlands on a plateau 7,300 feet (2,225m) above sea level, and ringed by majestic, snow-covered volcanoes and mountains. Originally built on the shores of the now long-vanished Lake Texcoco, the city is land-locked. It is the largest metropolis in the world, a mass of wide boulevards, narrow streets, parks and gardens divided into *colonias*.

In the centre of the city is the **Plaza de la Constitución** (Constitution Square), often referred to as the **Zócalo**, and the largest city square in the Americas. Built on the site of the Aztec capital Tenochtitlán, it is surrounded by over 1,400 historical buildings, reflecting 300 years of colonial splendour when Mexico City was referred to as the 'city of palaces'. Taking up two sides of the square is the **Metropolitan Cathedral** which took 250 years to complete, and the **Palacio Nacional**, once the palace of Cortés, then the residence of the Spanish Viceroys and now the official residence of the president.

A 24-square-block area at the eastern end of **Bosque de Chapultepec** (Chapultepec Park), known as the **Zona Rosa** (the Pink Zone), houses most of the hotels as well as some of the country's best shops, restaurants, pavement cafés, pedestrian malls, art galleries and book shops. Nightlife is centred in bars, clubs and discos, and leading hotels arrange entertainment in the form of Mexican *fiesta* nights, with cabaret and dancing.

Paseo de la Reforma is the main artery of the city and was modelled by French architects on the style of the Champs-Elysées in Paris, at the behest of Emperor Maximilian. It runs from Plaza de la Constitución to the castle in Chapultepec Park, which he converted into his imperial residence and which is now open to visitors. The park, with its walkways, botanical gardens, large lake and zoo, is a favourite meeting place for Mexicans.

WHAT TO SEE

Castles, Palaces, Historic Mansions and Monuments

◆

CASA DE LOS AZULEJOS (HOUSE OF TILES)
Avenida Madero 4
Believed to have been built by the son of a Count of Valle de Orizaba. Told by his father he was an idle young man and would never be able to afford a house of tiles, the son changed his ways and then built this house from the wealth he earned, covering its façade with blue and white tiles. It now houses a restaurant, and artefacts are sold in the gallery.

◆◆◆

CASTILLO DE CHAPULTEPEC (CHAPULTEPEC CASTLE)
Chapultepec Park
Close to the entrance to the park, the castle was begun in

1785, and became the imperial palace of Maximilian, later serving as a presidential home. In 1847 it was one of the last strongholds of the Mexicans during the United States invasion, stoutly defended by the Boy Heroes. The castle houses interesting carriages and the National Museum of History (see below).

◆

MONUMENTO A CUAUHTÉMOC (STATUE OF CUAUHTÉMOC)
Intersection of Paseo de la Reforma and Avenida Insurgentes Sur
Cuauhtémoc was the last Aztec emperor who fought fearlessly against the Spaniards and is held in high regard and affection by the Mexican people. Depicted on the base are scenes from his life.

◆◆

MONUMENTO A LA INDEPENDENCIA (INDEPENDENCE COLUMN)
Paseo de la Reforma
Called *El Angel*, the golden figure on top of the 118-foot (36m) high column depicts the goddess of liberty. At the base are statues of famous citizens connected with the independence movement.

◆

PALACIO DE ITURBIDE (ITURBIDE PALACE)
Avenida Madero 17
Originally the imperial house of Agustín de Iturbide, who nominated himself Emperor Agustín I when he became ruler of independent Mexico in

El Angel *was erected to celebrate Mexico's struggle for independence*

the 17th century. After losing the militia's backing Iturbide was banished in 1823 and having failed in an attempted return to power, he was eventually executed by a firing squad. Today his palace, designed by the famous architect Francisco Guerrero y Torres, is owned by the National Bank of Mexico.

◆◆◆

PALACIO NACIONAL (THE NATIONAL PALACE)
Plaza de la Constitución
On the eastern side of the

Plaza known as the Zócalo, the Palace was built in 1692 on the site of the Palace of Moctezuma. It houses the President's offices. Murals by Diego Rivera, at the top of the staircase and around the balcony on the first floor, colourfully present the history of Mexico. See also the 'Freedom Bell', above the central balcony, which is rung on Independence Day. It comes from the town of Dolores Hidalgo and was rung by Father Miguel Hidalgo to summon village folk to his church at the start of the War of Independence in 1810.
Open: daily: 07.00–19.00hrs.

◆◆
PLAZA DE LAS TRES CULTURAS (PLAZA OF THE THREE CULTURES)
Unidad-Nonoako-Tlatelolco
The market square of old Tlatelolco, where the Aztecs fought their last battle against the army of Hernán Cortés. Seen here, representing three cultures, are the ruins of an

CENTRO DE LA CIUDAD DEL MÉXICO

Aztec ceremonial centre, a Spanish Colonial 16th-century church, and the contemporary Foreign Ministry building, all on the same plaza.

Churches and Temples

♦♦♦

BASILÍCA DE GUADALUPE
Calzada Misterios
Near Insurgentes Norte on the northern outskirts of the city, the basilica is built on the spot where the Virgin Mary is said to have appeared in 1531 before a lowly Indian called

Juan Diego. It houses the most important religious painting in Mexico. Take the inexpensive Ruta 2 Minibus from the stop by the Independence Column and go to the end depot.

♦♦♦

CATEDRAL METROPOLITANA (METROPOLITAN CATHEDRAL)
Plaza de la Constitución Localo,
It took 250 years to complete the cathedral, which was

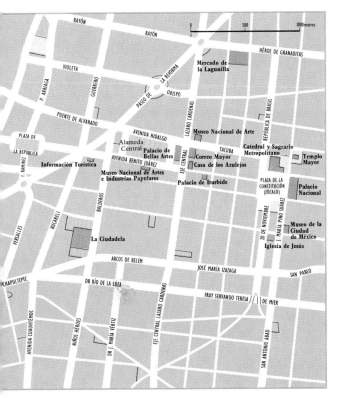

The Cathedral and Sagrado Metropolitano stand on a ruined Aztec temple

started in 1573 using many of the stones from the main temple of the Aztecs in Tenochtitlán. Within are 16 chapels and 21 altars. Note the twist in the main naves, due to the fact that the Spaniards filled in the Aztec canals and lake, and the foundations are now sinking.

◆
IGLESIA DE JESÚS NAZARO Y HOSPITAL (JESUS OF NAZARETH CHURCH AND HOSPITAL)
República del Salvador and Pino Suárez
Three blocks south of the main square stands the house of Hernán Cortés, where a plaque commemmorates his first meeting with Moctezuma. The hospital, founded in 1524,

was the first to be built in Mexico, now completely renovated.

◆◆
TEMPLO MAYOR (GREAT TEMPLE)
Seminario
The ruins on the northeast side of the Metropolitan Cathedral were rediscovered in 1978. Quantities of artefacts were found, including an eight ton/tonne carved monolith to the moon goddess, now in the National Museum of Archaeology. Templo Mayor has its own Museum.

◆◆◆
TEOTIHUACÁN (CITY OF THE GODS)
The ruins of this great city lie 30 miles (48 km) northeast of

Mexico City. Here is to be seen one of the finest Mesoamerican architectural sites in Mexico. Covering over eight square miles, the ruins are dominated by the great Pyramids of the Sun and Moon. It is best to go during the week, as residents of Mexico City crowd there at weekends. Sound and light shows take place from October to May.

Museums and Art Galleries

◆◆◆
BOSQUE DE CHAPULTEPEC (CHAPULTEPEC PARK)
Walking in the 'Forest of Grasshoppers' is a popular pastime, not only for visitors but also for residents of the city. On Sunday afternoons many local people picnic in this largest and oldest metropolitan park in the Americas. It contains eight museums, and three lakes, where you can take out a rowing boat. There is also a zoo and an amusement park. The zoo has 2,600 animals – over 300 species. It is a good place to take children, as there is a special area where they can get close to cubs and baby elephants as well as enjoy donkey rides and climb up tree houses.

◆◆
CIUDAD UNIVERSITARIA (UNIVERSITY CITY)
Cerro de Pedregal
Eight miles (13km) south of the Zócalo, the University's splendid wall murals and buildings, many of which incorporate Mesoamerican art forms, are well worth visiting, particularly for those interested in architecture.

◆◆
THE FLOATING GARDENS OF XOCHIMILCO
Xochimilco, some 15 miles (24km) southeast of the city centre
In Aztec times, when Mexico City was a waterborne city, rafts covered with soil were used to grow flowers and vegetables. In more recent times frameworks of sticks and clay were built in the lake shallows attached to the shore, and as the roots of the plants grew through the framework they anchored on the lake bottom, so forming the floating gardens. Today visitors travel through the remaining canals on gondolas, while other boats carrying *mariachi* players and *taco* vendors float by. Weekend traffic is heavy.

◆◆
MUSEO DE BELLAS ARTES (MUSEUM OF FINE ARTS)
Avenida Juárez
Housed in the splendid Art Nouveau Palacio de Bellas Artes, which is also the name of the national theatre and opera and the famous Folklórico Ballet, the museum displays murals by famous Mexican artists: Camarena, O'Gorman, Orozco, Sigueiros and Tamayo. The second version of Rivera's *Man at the Crossroads* is here, the original of which was in the Rockefeller Centre before it was painted over because of its Marxist bias.
The palace, made of white Carrara marble, features a

magnificent Tiffany glass mosaic curtain.

◆ MUSEO DE CERA (WAX MUSEUM)
Londres 6

Worth visiting for amusement. Usual formula of wax models of famous Mexicans and world history figures, plus a chamber of horrors, including Aztec human sacrifices.

◆◆ MUSEO DE LA CIUDAD DE MÉXICO (MEXICO CITY MUSEUM)
Pino Suárez 30

Prior to being rebuilt in the 18th century this manor belonged to the Counts of Santiago de Calimaya and dates back to 1528. Fine exhibits trace the history of Mexico City from pre-Columbian times to the present day.

◆◆◆ MUSEO NACIONAL DE ANTROPOLOGÍA (NATIONAL MUSEUM OF ANTHROPOLOGY)
Chapultepec Park

One of the finest exhibitions of its kind in the world. It is essential to visit prior to going on a classical tour. Provides a superb background history of Mesoamerica as well as housing great sculptures from the past. There are 25 rooms of exhibits (13 of archaeology and 12 devoted to ethnography). Multilingual guides are available, and there is an excellent bookshop.

◆◆ MUSEO NACIONAL DE ARTE (NATIONAL ART MUSEUM)
Tacuba 8

Near the main post office, the museum displays works of art by Mexican artists throughout history. Of particular significance is the fine bronze statue, by Manuel Tolsa, of *El Caballito*, the little horse that carried Charles IV of Spain.

This statue from Tula symbolises Quetzalcoatl as the morning star

◆
MUSEO NACIONAL DE ARTE MODERNO (NATIONAL MUSEUM OF MODERN ART)
Chapultepec Park
The museum houses a permanent exhibition of the works of many of the great post-independence artists of Mexico.

◆◆
MUSEO NACIONAL DE ARTES Y INDUSTRIAS POPULARES (NATIONAL MUSEUM OF FOLK ART)
Avenida Juárez 44
Shows the best works of modern craftsmen and artists throughout Mexico. Housed in a former convent, it is government-controlled. You can purchase such items as glass and copperware, pottery and woven goods.

◆◆◆
MUSEO NACIONAL DE HISTORIA (NATIONAL MUSEUM OF HISTORY)
Chapultepec Castle, Chapultepec Park
Describes Mexico's history, from the arrival of the conquistadores through to the Mexican Revolution. There are excellent murals by famous Mexican artists, including Juan O'Gorman, José Orozco and David Siquieros. Don't miss seeing the imperial apartments of Carlota and Maximilian, and the Gallery of Mexican History, designed for children.

◆◆
MUSEO DE TEMPLO MAYOR (MUSEUM OF TEMPLO MAYOR)
Seminario
Opened in 1987, the museum

Rivera's mural in the Palacio Nacional commemorates Aztec culture

contains many findings from the excavation of the Great Aztec Temple, and is adjacent to the same site. The most important display is of the Coyolxauhui Stone, representing the legend of the dismembered goddess.

◆◆
MUSEO TAMAYO (TAMAYO MUSEUM)
Paseo de la Reforma
In the park on the west side of the Reforma. Contains Tamayo's works, perhaps the doyen of Mexican modernists, plus those of other outstanding artists.

MEXICO CITY AND ENVIRONS

Accommodation

Mexico City offers everything from the ultra-modern, Super Deluxe hotels of the Zona Rosa or overlooking Chapultepec Park to small colonial-style hotels in less fashionable areas. Motels and guest houses are also in abundance. The price of hotels varies according to their standards. Because of sometimes quite rapid inflation it is best to check these prices before departure, but on the whole the Super Deluxe category of hotels may be 25 per cent lower in cost than its European equivalent. The classifications used are about equivalent to those in use in Europe and North America.

Super Deluxe

Camino Real (700 rooms) Mariano Escobedo 700 (tel: 203-2121).

María Isabel Sheraton (850 rooms) Paseo de la Reforma 325 (tel: 211-0001).

Nikko México (750 rooms) Campos Elíseos 204 (tel: 203-4020).

Moderate

The **Gran Hotel Ciudad de México** at Avenida 16 de Septiembre 82, (tel: 510-4040), is a charming, sophisticated and gracious hotel with 124 rooms. It has a palatial turn-of-the-century air with its crystal chandeliers, cage elevators and brass lamps. The rates are reasonable.

The **Marco Polo** at Amberes 27, (tel: 511-1839), is situated in the Zona Rosa's smartest street. It is a small establishment with 64 tastefully furnished rooms and four penthouse suites, offering personal service.

Other options include:

Airport Fiesta Americana (270 rooms) Boulevard Aeropuerto (tel: 762-0199).

Airport Holiday Inn (325 rooms) Boulevard Aeropuerto (tel: 762-4088).

Aristos (276 rooms) Paseo de la Reforma 276 (tel: 211-0112) Zona Rosa.

Calinda Geneve (352 rooms) Londres 130 (tel: 211-0071) Zona Rosa.

Century (142 rooms) Liverpool at Amberes (tel: 584-7111) Zona Rosa.

Gran Hotel Ciudad de México still has the grandeur of earlier times

Crowne Plaza Holiday Inn (546 rooms) Paseo de la Reforma 80 (tel: 566-7777).
Flamingos Plaza (256 rooms) Avenida de la Revolucíon 333 (tel: 271-7044).
Galeríe Plaza (434 rooms) Corner of Hamburgo and Varsovia (tel: 211-0014) Zona Rosa.
Krystal Rosa (328 rooms) Liverpool 155 (tel: 211-0092) Zona Rosa.
Plaza Florencia (130 rooms) Florencia 61 (tel: 533-6540).
Reforma (300 rooms) Paseo de la Reforma and Paris (tel: 546-9885)
Royal (162 rooms) Amberes 78 (tel: 525-4850) Zona Rosa.
Ritz (125 rooms) Madero 30 (tel: 518-1340)
Romano Diana Río Lerma 237 (tel: 211-0109).
Sevilla Palace (414 rooms) Paseo de la Reforma 105 (tel: 566-8877).
Stouffer Presidente Chapultepec (800 rooms) Campos Elíseos 218 (tel: 250-7700).

Inexpensive
Bristol (150 rooms) Plaza Nacaxa 17 (tel: 533-6060)
Corinto (155 rooms) Vallerta 24 (tel: 566-6555)
Del Angel (100 rooms) Río Lerma 154 (tel: 533-1032)
Diplomatico (107 rooms) Insurgentes Sur 1105 (tel: 563-6066)
El Ejecutivo (118 rooms) Viena 8 (tel: 566-6422)
María Cristina (146 rooms) Lerma 31 (tel: 546-9880)
Metropol (165 rooms) Luis Moya 39 (tel: 510-8660).
Prim (160 rooms) Versailles 46

(tel: 592-1609)
Plaza Reforma (104 rooms) Insurgentes Centro 149 (tel: 546-4540)
Vasco de Quiroga (50 rooms) Londres 15 (tel: 546-2614)

Economy
Edison (45 rooms) Edison 106 (tel: 566-0933)
Fleming (75 rooms) Revillagigedo 35 (tel: 510-4530)
Isabel (74 rooms) Isabel de la Católica 63 (tel: 518-1213)
Monte Carlo (59 rooms) Uruguay 69 (tel: 585-1222)
Panuco (60 rooms) Ayuntamento 148 (tel: 585-1355).

Markets and Craft Centres
There is a plentiful supply of interesting products to buy in Mexico (see **Shopping**, page 104). Mexico City has innumerable places where craft stalls are set up, paintings are on display by local artists and flowers and fruit are for sale. Prices are cheap compared with those in Europe.
Among the leading centres are the **Mercado de la Merced** the biggest market in Mexico, which is to be found on Anillo de Circunvaluacíon.
Bazaar Sábado at the Plaza San Jacinto-Villa Obregón in San Ángel is the place for high quality workmanship. It is open on Saturdays only.
Mercado de la Lagunilla on Calle Rayón sells absolutely everything. It is open on Saturday mornings.
El Artesanal Buenavista, behind the Buenavista railway station in a splendid building at Ayuntamiento 70, is another

large market for handicrafts, including jewellery. These venues are very busy and colourful, and you are expected to haggle over the quoted cost.

Nightlife

Nearly all of Mexico City's larger hotels have night-clubs and many discotheques, hence a lot of the action is centered around the Zona Rosa (Pink Zone). About 22.00hrs is a good time to visit restaurants and dance spots, and most shows don't begin before midnight, despite what they might say on the programme. It is advisable to book in advance. Nearly all restaurants and night-clubs are closed on Sundays.

A good way to see some of the night spots outside of the hotels is to take a tour, which can be arranged at most hotel reception desks. These provide an opportunity to meet other people and to see what the city's nightlife has to offer – and it can also save you money.

If you want to explore, head for the Plaza de Garibaldi. It is here that the *mariachis* hang out – bands of musicians playing loud, exuberant music, dressed in traditional tight jackets, studded with silver buttons, and wide sombreros.

Discos start about 20.00hrs and finish around 04.00hrs, and usually have a cover charge. A cross section includes **Can Can** on the corner of Calle Hamburgo and Calle Genova, **Cero-Cero** in Hotel Camino Real; **Disco Club 84** in the Stouffer Presidente

Chapultepec; **El Señorial** at Hamburgo 188, off Florencia; **Le Chic** in the Galería Plaza Hotel; **News** at Av San Jerónimo 252; **Verandah Bar** in the María Isabel Sheraton; and **Zazzy** in the Nikko Hotel.

Dinner and Dancing (prices vary): a cross section includes **Chez 'Ar** in the Hotel Aristos, with live music and Mediterranean décor; **Muralto** on 41st floor of the Latin American Tower, with excellent views of the city at night, and **Restaurant del Lago** in Chapultepec Park overlooking nearby lake.

Night-clubs

Most shows take place twice nightly, at 23.00 and 01.00hrs. Below is a selection of some clubs:

Barbarella, Holiday Inn, Crowne Plaza, has two floor shows and **El Corral de la Moreria**, Londres 161, features Flamenco dancing. **El Patio**, Atenas 9, shows on the grand scale featuring national and international headliners, while **Fiesta Mexicana**, Hotel Cortés, on Saturday night features a charming Mexican folkloric show, as does **Plaza Santa Cecilia**, off Garibaldi Square, where there is a cover charge so that you can dine or just enjoy drinks. **Marrakesh**, Florencia 36, has four clubs in one including disco and nightclub with top quality floorshow, and **Stelaris**, top floor of the Crowne Palace Hotel, with its highly regarded supper club with dancing and floor show, overlooks city lights.

Night entertainment abounds in
Mexico City. Fuller information
and up-to-date prices can be
obtained from a weekly
publication called *Tiempo Libre*.
New editions are available at
newstands on Fridays.

*The flagstoned courtyard of an old
hacienda is a cool and relaxing
place to eat traditional food*

Restaurants
There is a vast range of
restaurants in Mexico City,
many serving Mexican food
and others specialising in
different cuisines from around
the world. A large number of
restaurants feature a tourist
menu at a nominal price which
also includes a cocktail or
wine. Mexicans eat their main
meal at lunchtime and
restaurants get busy around
14.00hrs, so if you want a
leisurely meal and to avoid the
rush, it's advisable to eat about
13.00hrs.

The **Centre** is probably the
best place for good variety at
reasonable prices. For more
expensive tastes you should
try **Antigua Hacienda de
Tlalpan** at Calzada de Tlalpan,
which specialises in fine
Mexican and international
cuisine. **Delmónico's**, in the

Zona Rosa, is also famous for its excellent cuisine.

Sports and Activities

On Sundays bullfights or *Corrida*, take place in the world's largest bullring, **Plaza México**, on Insurgentes Sur (*Metro*: San Antonio - Line 7). Bullfights begin at 16.00hrs. Make sure you book a seat in the shade. The best time is December to March. Tickets from most hotel desks. Rodeos, or *Charreada* are a popular activity for Mexicans and Charro associations arrange these usually on Sunday morning. Many are held at the **Rancho del Charro**, on the western side of Chapultepec Park, or at the **Lienzo del Charro** in Pedregal, on the south side of the city. Soccer or *fútbol* enthusiasts will find this game has a huge following. Games usually take place at weekends throughout the year at the **Azteca Stadium** on the south side of the city (scene of the 1986 World Cup Final), the **Sports City Stadium** (Magdalena Mixuca) near the bullring or the **Olympic Stadium** in University City. The longest racing season in the world is held at the **Hipódromo de las Américas** on Avenida Avila Camacho, and races start at 14.30hrs on weekends and at 15.00hrs on Tuesday, Thursday and Friday. Bets can be placed at under a dollar. You can dine at the Derby Club and watch the races at the same time. One of the most exciting sports to watch is *jai alai*, the Basque variety of handball which uses wicker basket gloves to hurtle the ball at breathtaking speeds. This can be seen every evening except Monday and Friday at the **Frontón México** on the Plaza de la República (*Metro*: Revolucíon - Line 2). Games begin about 19.00hrs, and the programme explains the finer points of the sport in English.

Transport

Shared **taxis** called *peseros* (only a peso once upon a time, hence the name), are cheap and operate on fixed routes. Taxis are reasonably priced but at night the meters are not used. They display a *sitio* sign. Unmarked *turismo* limousines, usually found outside hotels are useful for sightseeing and prices by the hour can be negotiated in advance.

Buses are cheap and depart from four outlying termini. The principal routes run along the Reforma, Juárez and Madero and from Chapultepec Park to the Zócalo. The subway system (**Metro**) is one of the best anywhere and, again, fares cost only a few pesos. The stations are clean and well lit, some playing classical music, and colour-keyed signs define the different routes. Trains operate between 06.00hrs and midnight.

Some forty **coach** tour operators run sightseeing tours around the city and to surrounding sites and the bigger hotels have information desks which can provide the visitor with useful data on places to see and times of coach departures.

CENTRAL MEXICO

CUERNAVACA

Lying about 50miles (80km) south of Mexico City is the capital of the state of Morelos. In Mesoamerican times the Indians called it Cuauhnáchuac, which to Spanish ears sounded like *cuerno de vaca* (cow's horn), and that is how the town came to be named. The altitude here is 2,000 feet (609m) lower than the capital and the temperature is balmy throughout the year. The Aztec nobility wintered here, Hernán Cortés built a palace, and Emperor Maximilian vacationed in an 18th-century mansion built by the silver magnate, José de la Borda. Today the tropical flowers and garden restaurants continue to attract the visitor away from the bustling crowds of Mexico City, either for the day or weekend.

WHAT TO SEE

◆
CATHEDRAL
Avenida Hidalgo
Started in 1529 and hence one of the Old Mexican churches. Recently discovered murals depict scenes of martyrdom of missionaries who sailed to Japan in the 16th century.

◆
JARDÍN BORDA (BORDA GARDENS)
Built by a silver magnate of the same name who struck it rich, the magnificent mansion and gardens have been restored. Borda was fond of formal gardens and built numerous pools, fountains and terraces. There are frequent art exhibitions and concerts.

◆◆◆
PALACIO DE CORTÉS (PALACE OF CORTÉS)
Built by the Zócalo, the palace was begun in 1530 and today

CENTRAL MEXICO

Little is known about the people who built the fortress city at Xochicalco

houses the **Museo de Cuauhnáhuac** (Museum of Cuauhnáhuac) which contains colonial furniture, historical exhibits and Diego Rivera murals recounting events in Mexican history.

◆
PYRAMID OF TEOPANZOLCO
Avenida Río Balsas
Near the railway station are the only Aztec remains in Cuernavaca.

◆◆◆
XOCHICALCO
A large defensible site handsomely restored, lying on the steep terraced hills of Morelos, one hour's drive to the southwest of Cuernavaca.

Accommodation
Two lovely *haciendas* in the Cuernavaca area have been converted into hotels. They are **Hacienda de Cocoyoc**, Cuatla Highway (tel: 735-2-2000), 20 miles (32km) to the east, and **Hacienda Vista Hermosa**, Tequesquintengo (tel: 734-3-0300), 15 miles (24km) south. Both are in the Deluxe category.

Moderate
The **Posada Las Mañanitas**, at Ricardo Liñares 107 (tel: 12-4646) is well known for its delightful tropical gardens where parrots, flamingoes and peacocks are in residence. The facilities include an excellent dining room, cocktail lounge and heated swimming pool.
The 38-room **Villa del Conquistador** at Paseo del Conquistador 134 (tel: 13-1055), has a splendid view of Cuernavaca. As well as two

restaurants and a bar with live entertainment, there are facilities for a variety of sports including swimming, squash, and miniature golf.
Others include:
Hotel Casino de la Selva (228 rooms) Leandro Valle 1001 (tel: 12-4700)
Las Quintas (46 rooms) Avenida Las Quintas 107 (tel: 12-8800).
Posada de Xochiquetzal (14 rooms) Calle Leyva 200 (tel: 12-0220)
Posada Jacarandas (90 rooms) Cuauhtémoc 805 (tel: 15-7777).
Racquet Club (36 rooms) Francisco Villa 100 (tel: 13-6122)

Inexpensive
OK Inn (46 rooms) Emiliano Zapata 825 (tel: 13-1270).
Palacio (16 rooms) Calle Morrow 204 (tel: 12-0553)
Papagayo (90 rooms) Motolinia 13 (tel: 12-4694)

Night-clubs
Cuernavaca is a lively place at weekends and nightspots are to be found in the Hacienda de Cocoyoc and the Hotel Casino de la Selva and there are several discos open at weekends which include **Barba Azul**, Prado 10, **Kaova**, Leyva 10, and **Maximiliano's**, Juan Ruiz de Alarcon 7.

Restaurants
Include **La India Bonito Morrow**, for excellent Mexican food at a reasonable price. For dining out in style there is **Le Château René**, Atzingo 11, and **Las Mañanitas**, Ricardo Linares 107, with an international menu in a fine setting.

TAXCO

This oldest silver mining town in Mexico rests on the side of a mountain, some 50 miles (80km) to the southwest of Cuernavaca. Much of Colonial Taxco is paved with cobble-stones, and nearly all the houses have red-tile roofs. 'Tlalco', the original name for the town means 'a place where they play'. The beautiful baroque church of Santa Prisca y San Sebastián dominates the centre, especially at night, when it is floodlit. Taxco is full of shops selling well-crafted silver jewellery and *objets d'art*. If you are buying an expensive item, look for the hallmark – .925 – the government's requirement for purity in silver.

WHAT TO SEE

◆
CASA HUMBOLDT
Calle Juan Ruiz de Alarcón
It is a beautiful mansion, Moorish in design and originally an inn lying between the capital and Acapulco. It takes its name from the well-known 19th-century German traveller to these parts, Alexander Von Humboldt. Now sells interesting handicrafts from all over the state of Guerrero.

◆◆◆
IGLESIA DE SAN SEBASTIÁN Y SANTA PRISCA (CHURCH OF SANTA PRISCA)
The church has magnificent spires, a colourful dome and Churrigueresque style of interior which is the hallmark of 18th-century colonial

architecture. Don't miss the fine paintings of Miguel Cabrera, one of the leading artists of this period.

♦

MUSEO GUILLERMO SPRATLING (SPRATLING MUSEUM)

Behind the main church is an exhibition of silver articles going back to the Mesoamerican period as well as models of colonial mines.

Accommodation

Moderate

Posada de la Misión on Avenida J F Kennedy (tel: 2-0063) is a converted old Spanish mission, decorated in colonial style. Most of its 105 rooms are on the small side, but there are some larger suites available.
Facilities include a bar, disco, jacuzzi and tennis court and there is a fine Juan O'Gorman mural alongside the pool. Rates are moderate.
Others include:
De la Borda (150 rooms) Cerro del Pedregal 2 (tel: 2-0025).
Hacienda del Solar (17 rooms) Off highway 95 south of town (tel: 2-0323).
Monte Taxco (160 rooms) Lomas de Taxco (tel: 2-1300).
Rancho Taxco-Victoria (100 rooms) Carlos J Nibbi 5 (tel: 2-0210).

Inexpensive

Los Arcos (tel: 2-1836) is just a stone's throw from the Zócalo, at Juan Ruiz de Alarcón 12. Its handsome, whitewashed rooms are situated round a cool courtyard and small fountain, and are reasonably priced. There is a small pool, piano

bar, restaurant and rooftop terrace with a great view of the town.
Others include:
Loma Linda (90 rooms) Avenida John F Kennedy 52 (tel: 2-0206).
Los Castillo (15 rooms) Juan Ruiz de Alarcón 3 (tel: 2-1396).
Santa Prisca (40 rooms) Cena Obscuras 1 (tel: 2-0080).

Nightlife

This can be found in the Cantarranas night-club called **La Jungla**, with Mexican-Indian show and fireworks. It lies just south of Taxco. Other discos – **Bugambillas** at Juan Ruiz de Alarcón 7; **El Jumil** in the Hotel Monte Taxco and **Tropica** on the Plaza. Many lively restaurants around the main cathedral, crowded with artists and writers from many parts of the world. Menu prices range from moderately expensive at the **Ventana de Taxco** south of the town, which is famous for its Italian dishes and gourmet cuisine, to the inexpensive at the **Bora** overlooking the Zócalo, and **Restaurant La Hacienda** on Plaza Borda 4, which serves delicious Mexican meals.

PUEBLA

Puebla is two hours' drive southeast of Mexico City in the foothills of the Sierra Madre with several spectacular extinct volcanoes on its skyline. The town was built as a Spanish stronghold soon after the Conquest and it was here that a small Mexican army of 2,000 men defeated a French army three times its number.

Its long history as a ceramic centre dates back to pre-Columbian times and today it is often referred to as the 'City of Tiles'. You will see the use of hand-wrought Talavera tiles all over the city, on churches and administrative buildings and patios. You can buy tiles from the many factory shops.

Santo Domingo, Puebla, is among the best examples of Mexican baroque

WHAT TO SEE

♦♦♦
CATHEDRAL OF THE IMMACULATE CONCEPTION
on the Zócalo
The cathedral with the tallest towers in Mexico is notable for its carved façade, fourteen chapels and its dome decorated with the local *azulejos* tiles.

♦♦
IGLESIA SANTO DOMINGO (CHURCH OF SANTO DOMINGO)
5 de Mayo
Dating from 1611, the church is worth seeing for its Rosary Chapel with its jewelled Virgin and walls of carved wood figures, gold leaf and tiles.

♦
MUSEO DE ARTE JOSÉ LUIS BELLO Y GONZALEZ (BELLO MUSEUM)
3 Pontiente 302
The museum has some interesting pictures by colonial artists as well as a collection of colonial furniture. Closed on Mondays.

♦♦♦
PYRAMID OF CHOLULA
Five miles (8km) west of Puebla
Cholula became the most important city in the Valley of Mexico after the demise of Teotihuacán. The pyramid dedicated to Quetzalcóatl is the largest single structure in the Americas. It has been enlarged four times since its original size. It is now 181 feet (55m) high and covers 40 acres (16 hectares). The site which has been influenced by Olmec, Teotihuacános and Toltec civilisations has been extensively excavated to expose stairs and plazas. Inside are miles of tunnels. Don't miss the colourful murals of the *bebedores*. The pyramid is partly covered by a 230-foot (70m) hill upon which stands the church, Nuestra Señora de los Remedios.

♦♦♦
SANTA MARÍA TONANTZINTLA
Nine miles (14km) from Puebla
A marvellous example of how Indian artists interpreted Biblical teaching and their ability to adapt their art and skills from Mesoamerican architectural requirements to European.

Accommodation

Moderate
Generally considered to be the best place in town is **El Méson del Angel** at Avenida Hermanos Serdán 807 (tel: 48-2100). This 200-room hotel on the edge of town has landscaped grounds and good views of the volcanoes. Recreational facilities include a bowling alley, tennis courts and two pools. Moderately priced.
Others include:
Aristos (120 rooms) Reforma and Calle 7 (tel: 42-5982).
Campestre Los Sauces (40 rooms) between Puebla and Cholula (tel: 47-1011).
Misión de Puebla (225 rooms) 5 Poniente 252 (tel: 48-9600).
Villa Arqueológica (40 rooms) 2 Poniente 601, Cholula (tel: 47-1966)

Inexpensive
The **Posada San Pedro**, at 2 Oriente 202 (tel: 46-5077), is a colonial-style hotel downtown. It has a small open-air swimming pool and two restaurants. Rooms, though a little small, are quite pleasant and reasonably priced.
Others include:
Cabrera (60 rooms) 10 Oriente 6 (tel: 41-8525).
Gilfer (90 rooms) 2 Oriente 11 (tel: 40-6611)
Lastra (55 rooms) Calzada de los Fuertes 2633 (tel: 35-9755).
Palacio de Puebla (48 rooms) 2 Oriente 13 (tel: 41-2430).
Palacio San Leonardo (74 rooms) 2 Oriente 211 (tel: 48-0555).
Royalty (46 rooms) Portal Hidalgo 8 (tel: 42-4740).

Virrey de Mendoza (18 rooms) 3 Poniente 912 (tel: 42-3903).

Nightlife
Includes the **D'Artagnan** at Juárez 2923, **Midae** in Cholula, and **Porthos** on the Cholula Road. Both the **Mesón del Angel** and the **Misión** hotels feature a dinner show at the weekends, as does **Flamingos** at Teziutlán Norte 1. Several moderately priced restaurants include **D'Armando's**, **Charlie's China Poblano**, **Gran Tasco**, **La Cava de los Angeles** and **Tio Max** all in the new chic Emerald Zone on Av Juárez. The **Fenda de Santa Clara**, west of the Zócalo, features some great regional delicacies, including *mole poblano*, Puebla's speciality chocolate sauce.

INDEPENDENCE ROUTE

In exploring the heart of Mexico, a worthwhile trip, either privately by car or on a coach tour, is to follow the Independence Route that traces Mexico's struggle for liberty via Spanish colonial towns and villages on a 475 mile (764km) circular journey west and north of the capital.

QUERÉTARO

Lies two hours' drive north of the capital. It was taken over by the Spanish in 1531 and many beautiful churches were built here during the colonial period. It also became important during the fight for independence and the venue where Mexico's Constitution was prepared and signed. Together with nearby **Juan del Río** and **Tequisquiapan** (a thermal spa) the area has become the gem-cutting and polishing centre of Mexico, and here is the place to make your jewellery purchase.

Querétaro has beautiful colonial buildings set in parks and plazas

WHAT TO SEE

◆

MUSEO REGIONAL DE QUERÉTARO (REGIONAL MUSEUM)

Juárez Street

Originally a 17th-century convent, it now contains colonial furniture including the table where Mexico had to sign away large territories west of the Mississippi after the Mexican War, plus other historical memorabilia.

◆◆◆

TULA

Reached by Highway 57, which runs north from Mexico City to Querétaro. Most important Toltec site and former capital of that empire.

Accommodation

Moderate

Hacienda Jurica situated north of town, off Highway 57 (tel: 2-1081), is a 186-room hotel, built around a splendid 17th-century hacienda and offering a wide variety of recreational facilities, including swimming, golf, tennis and horse riding.

The **Real de Minas** on Constituyentes 124 Poniente, south of Highway 57 (tel: 6-0444), has over 200 comfortable rooms, each with wall-to-wall carpeting, air-conditioning, heating and TV. Among other amenities are a piano bar, night club and private dining rooms.

Others include:

Holiday Inn (172 rooms) Hwy 57, Av Constituyentes 13 Sur (tel: 6-0202).

Mesón de Santa Rosa (21 rooms) Pasteur Sur 17, Lapaza de Armas (tel: 2-0415)

Mirabel (171 rooms) Constituyentes 2 Oriente (tel: 4-3535)

Inexpensive

Azteca (45 rooms) Hwy 57 (tel: 2-2060).

Hotel El Senorial (45 rooms) Guerrero Norte 10A (tel: 4-3700).

Nightlife

There are several discos including **Zero's** at the Holiday Inn and the night-club **La Cava** at the Corregidora.

There are a number of indoor/outdoor restaurants from where you can watch passers-by, to **La Fontana**, for a more expensive international cuisine in luxury colonial décor. For excellent food at a reasonable price you should go to **La Flor de Querétaro**, at Juárez Norte 5.

SAN MIGUEL DE ALLENDE

One hour's drive further on from Querétaro is San Miguel de Allende, one of the few colonial towns designated a national monument and a favourite residential city for artists and writers from the USA who`come to live in Mexico. Founded in 1542 by a Franciscan monk, Juan de San Miguel, 'Allende' was added in honour of the revolutionary Ignacio Allende born here. He fought beside Hidalgo for Independence. Six thousand feet (1828m) up on the side of a mountain, this sleepy cobble-stoned colonial town with elegant houses, and tree-lined

Lively San Miguel attracts artists and writers as well as tourists

patios is a great attraction to visitors.

Accommodation

Moderate

The **Posada la Aldea** at Ancha de San Antonio (tel: 2-1296), has 66 rooms, all with bathrooms which feature interesting *azulejo* tiles and half overlook an enormous garden and courtyard with a fountain. There is a small restaurant with a fine view of the town, as well as a swimming pool, games rooms and TV room.

Others include:

Aristos Parador San Miguel (56 rooms) Calle Ancha de San Antonio (tel: 2-0149)

Casa de Sierra Nevada (20 rooms) Hospicio 35 (tel: 2-0415)

Hacienda de las Flores (10 suites, 23 rooms) Hospicio 16 (tel: 2-1808)

Hacienda Taboada (60 rooms) Dolores Hidalgo Highway (tel: 2-0850).

Rancho el Atascadero (51 rooms) also bungalows, Prolongacíon Santo Domingo (tel: 2-0337).

Villas El Molino (60 rooms) Salida Real a Querétaro (tel: 2-1818).

Inexpensive

La Mansion del Bosque on Aldama 65 Juárez Parl (tel: 2-0277), is small, intimate and charming. The 24 rooms vary in size but are all tastefully furnished. Rates include breakfast and dinner.

Misión de los Angeles (65 rooms) 1 mile (2km) along Hwy to Celaya (tel: 2-1026).

Economy

Mesón de San Antonio (16 rooms) Mesones 80 (tel: 2-0580)

Motel la Siesta (28 rooms) half a mile (1km) along Hwy to

CENTRAL MEXICO

Celaya (tel: 2-0207).
Posada Carmina (10 rooms)
Cuña de Allende 7 (tel: 2-0458).
Posada las Monjas (63 rooms)
Canal 37 (tel: 2-0171).
Posada San Francisco (40
rooms) Main Plaza (tel: 2-1466).
Quinta Loreto (28 rooms)
Callejon de Loreto 15 (tel:
2-0042).
Vista Hermosa (19 rooms) Cuña
de Allende II (tel: 2-0437).

Restaurants

Entertainment is mainly found
eating out in good restaurants
such as the **Mama Mía** or **La
Fragua**, which also have live
entertainment. Sea food is a
speciality of several places
such as **El Muelle** and **Chez
Max** and if you like a dinner
dance try **La Princesca**. The
cuisine is international and the
atmosphere dark and relaxing.

GUANAJUATO

An hour's drive from San
Miguel, Guanajuato is situated
in a canyon between two
sierras at 6,700 feet (2,042m). It
was a silver mining city and
the **Valenciana Mine** here was
one of the richest producing
ever known. The cobble-
stoned streets and stone steps
amid churches and plazas are
great for meandering. There is
a unique underground subway
for cars. Visit the **Jardín de la
Unión** (Garden of the Union), a
favourite promenade plaza
where band concerts are held.
Nearby is the **Teatro Juárez** to
which repertory companies,
symphony orchestras and
ballet schools from many
different countries are invited.
Near to the University, Diego

*Painted houses and narrow crooked
streets make Guanajuato attractive*

Rivera was born, and his house
is now a **museum** which
displays many of his early
sketches and paintings.

Accommodation

Moderate

The striking **Museo Posada
Santa Fe** is located on the
Jardín de la Unión (tel: 2-0084).
It is a charming, colonial-style
building which dates from the
mid-19th century, and has a
very popular outdoor café,
though service here can be
slow. The rooms are well kept
and comfortable and rates are
moderate.
Others include:
Castillo de Santa Cecilia (87
rooms) Hwy 110 to Dolores
Hidalgo (tel: 2-0573).

**Hotel Hacienda San Gabriel
Barrera** (139 rooms) Marfíl Hwy
(tel: 2-3980).
Parador San Javier (117 rooms)
Hwy 110, Aldama 92 (tel:
2-0626).
Paseo de la Presa (60 rooms)
Carretera Panoramica (tel:
2-3761)
Real de Minas (147 rooms)
Nejayote 17 (tel: 2-1460).

Inexpensive

Hotel San Francisco on Juárez
at Gavira (tel: 2-2084), is across
from the market, which can be
noisy. The rooms are pleasant
and rates are reasonable, but
ask for a room in the interior,
not off the balcony, as it will be
quieter here.
Others include:
El Conde (58 rooms) Rangel de
Alba No 1 (tel: 2-1465).
El Carruaje (50 rooms) Hwy

110 to Dolores Hidalgo (tel:
2-2140).
El Insurgente (82 rooms) Av
Juárez 224 (tel: 2-2294).
Embajadoras (27 rooms)
Parque Embajadoras (tel:
2-0081).
Hacienda de los Cobos (39
rooms) Padre Hidalgo (tel:
2-0350).
Hostería del Fraile (37 rooms)
Sopeña 3 (tel: 2-1179).
Mineral de Rayas (82 rooms)
Calle Alhondiga No 7 (tel:
2-0543).
Motel Guanajuato (50 units)
Hwy 110 to Dolores Hidalgo
(tel: 2-0689).
San Diego (55 rooms) Jardín de
la Unión No 1 (tel: 2-1300).
Valenciana (41 rooms) Hwy 110
to Dolores Hidalgo (tel: 2-0799).
Villa de la Plata (42 units) Hwy
110 to Dolores Hidalgo (tel:
2-5200).

Restaurants

In this area is a great variety in
terms of price and types of
cuisine, mainly in the hotels
themselves. **Las Palomas**, at
Calle de la Campana 19,
serves good Mexican food as
well as some Italian dishes, at
very reasonable prices.

MORELIA

Morelia is the capital of the
state of Michoacán and you
can now take a short flight or
drive on new highways from
Mexico City. The latter takes
four hours. By and large most
of the buildings belong to the
traditional style of New Spain.
The city was founded in 1541
by Antonio de Mendoza, the
first viceroy, and originally
called Valladolid. Its

CENTRAL MEXICO

The dome of Morelia Cathedral is covered with ceramic tiles or azulejos

impressive **Cathedral** constructed of slightly pink stone, with its 200-foot (60m) tower, dominates the **Plaza de los Martires**. The majority of the city's leading attractions are within a six-block radius of this centre-piece, which took some 200 years to build. Interesting places to see include the massive colonial **aqueduct** and the **Colegio de San Nicolás** (College of San Nicolas), the second oldest European educational institution in America. Morelia is noted for its lacquerware.

Accommodation

Moderate

The **Virrey de Mendoza** is conveniently located on the main plaza, at Portal de Matamoros 16 (tel: 2-0633).

Originally a private house, this colonial-style hotel has over 50 rooms with soaring ceilings, hanging lamps and four-poster beds. It offers good food and service at a reasonable price. Others include:

Alameda (75 rooms) Madero Poniente and Guillermo Prieto (tel: 2-2023).

Calinda Morelia Quality Inn (126 rooms) Av de la Camelinas (tel: 4-5969).

Misión Morelia (275 rooms) Av Ventura Puente (tel: 5-0023).

Posada de la Soledad (65 rooms) Zaragoza 90 (tel: 2-1888).

Real Victoria (111 rooms) Guadalupe Victoria 245 (tel: 3-2511).

Stouffer Presidente (90 rooms) Aquiles Serdan 647 (tel: 2-2626).

Villa del Sol (80 rooms)
Tecnológico 1811 (tel: 2-4034)
Villa Montaña (70 bungalows)
Calle Patzimba (tel: 4-0179).

Inexpensive

The **Catedral** on Ignacio
Zaragoza 37 (tel: 3-0783), is on
the Zócalo. Its light and airy
rooms, which are carpeted
and have huge bathrooms, are
arranged around a pleasant
courtyard. Amenities include a
café, restaurant and bar with
live entertainment.
Others include:
Hotel Valladolid (32 rooms)
Portal Hidalgo 241 (tel: 2-0027).

Restaurants

Most dining is in hotels or
centrally located restaurants
such as **Monterrey**, **La
Huacana**, **Los Canarios**, **La
Cabana**, **Los Comenzales** and
Grill de Eurique, although
there is a good selection of
restaurants which are not
actually in the centre such as
the **El Zaguan**, which
specialises in seafood dishes,
and the **Casa Paya** which
specialises in Spanish dishes.

PÁTZCUARO

Located in 150 miles (241km)
west of Mexico City at 7,000ft
(2,133m) above sea level and
just a couple of miles from
Lago de Pátzcuaro (Pátzcuaro
Lake), the city of Pátzcuaro
offers a relaxed atmosphere in
a lovely setting and the
opportunity to shop for a wide
and interesting variety of local
crafts.
Pine forests and lakes make
Pátzcuaro a very different
place for travellers and
vacationers who think of
Mexico in terms of heat, sun
and sand.
The main square in town is the
Plaza Vasco de Quiroga,
named after a 16th-century
bishop. **Plaza Gertrudis
Bocanegra** honours a heroine
and martyr of Mexico's
independence movement.
Nearby is a library with a
mural by Juan O'Gorman
depicting the history of the
Tarascan culture.
The lake is 55 miles (88km) in
circumference and contains a
number of islands, including
Janítzio, which is dominated by
a giant statue in memory of
José María Morelos, another
hero of the independence
movement.
Friday is market day at the
lakeshore, with vendors selling
fried fish. Pátzcuaro whitefish
and other lake fish are
specialities of the area. About
eight miles (12km) outside
Pátzcuaro are the ruins of
Tzintzúntzan. When the
Spaniards arrived in this
region, they estimated that
40,000 Tarascans lived in the
city of temples, palaces and
artisans' shops. The Tarascans
were well known for their skill
and artistry in metal work and
jewellery.
Friday is the main market day
for crafts, but many shops are
open every day. Pátzcuaro is
noted for lacquerware,
rebozos, *serapes*, sweaters,
straw items, *huaraches*,
copperware and handwoven
fabric.
Some of the nearby villages
specialise in different crafts,
especially ceramics.

WHAT TO SEE

◆

BASILÍCA DE NUESTRA SEÑORA DE LA SALUD (OUR LADY OF HEALTH)

Early colonial period with a revered 16th-century image of the Virgin made of corn paste.

◆

ISLAND OF JANÍTZIO

Contains monolith of José María Morelos larger than the Statue of Liberty. Independence ceremony held here on the eve of 1 November.

◆

MUSEO DE ARTES POPULARES (MUSEUM OF POPULAR ARTS)

Calle Alcantarillos
Houses a fine collection of ceramics, handicrafts, lacquerware and masks.

◆◆

TINGAMBATO

On the road to Uruapan
A former Tarascan ceremonial complex with a pyramid, two plazas and a ballcourt.

◆◆◆

TZINTZÚNTZAN

Eight miles (12km) along main road to Quiroga
The original capital of the Tarascan Indians. The archaeological ruins are distinctive and show five *yácatas*, or temple bases.

Accommodation

Moderate
Don Vosco (102 rooms) Av de las Américas 450 (tel: 2-0227).

Inexpensive
Mesón del Gallo at Dr José María Coss (tel: 2-1474), is an extremely well-maintained colonial mission-style hotel. The rooms are small but comfortable. Amenities include a pool and restaurant.
The **Posada de San Rafael** is on the main plaza at Plaza Vasco 18 (tel: 2-0770). It is a colonial-style inn with over 100 rooms surrounding a courtyard. Some rooms have wooden floors and beamed ceilings. Others include:
Gran Hotel (26 rooms) Portal Regules 6 (tel: 2-0443).
Hosteria San Felipe (12 rooms) Lazaro Cardenas 321 (tel: 2-1298).
Los Escudos (30 rooms) Portal Hidalgo 73 (tel: 2-0138).
Mesón del Cortijo (14 rooms) Prolongacíon Alvaro Obregon (tel: 2-1295)
Misión San Manuel (19 rooms) Plaza Vasco de Quiroga 12 (tel: 2-1313).
Posada de la Basílica (11 rooms) Arciga 6 (tel: 2-0770).

Economy
Valmen (17 rooms) Lloreda 34 (tel: 2-1161).

Restaurants

There is a selection of good restaurants serving excellent local dishes, such as the **Hosteria San Felipe** which lies between the town and the main hotel **Don Vasco**, **Los Escudos** at Portal Hidalgo 73, and **El Patio** on Plaza Vasco de Quiroga. **El Monje**, at the **Hotel Misíon San Manuel**, serves a large selection of soups and broths and a speciality called *chareles*. Visit the lakeside stands which sell the excellent whitefish caught here.

GUADALAJARA

The neoclassical Teatro Degollado in Guadalajara

Guadalajara has a population of 3.5 million people and is the second largest city in Mexico. Located on a mile-high (1.6km) plateau some 360 miles (580km) north-west of Mexico City, it is known as the 'City of Roses'. Many Americans live here because of the ideal climate. Trees, flowers and fountains decorate the city. Founded in 1541, the centre of the city is a fine example of Spanish Colonial architecture and is dominated by the **Cathedral** which is surrounded by four plazas. Good shopping areas include, the **Mercado Libertad**, **Casa de Las Artesanías de Jalisco**, **Plaza del Sol** or the nearby villages of **Tlaquepaque** and **Tonalá**. The latter is the region's premier centre for ceramics, and attractive fauna and flora designs are displayed on traditional burnished pottery. Of special interest is the **Teatro Degollado** (Degollado Theatre), with its vaulted ceiling decorated on themes from Dante's *Divine Comedy*. The work of the famous Mexican painter José Clemente Orozco figures prominently in Guadalajara. The **Palacio de Gobierno** (Government Palace) houses his masterpiece showing Hidalgo, the 'Father of Mexico's Independence', brandishing a fiery sword against a background of red flags and flames. In the **Hospico del Obispo Cabañas**, the artist has immortalised the Bishop Cabañas in the frescos with which he decorated the chapel; and more of his work

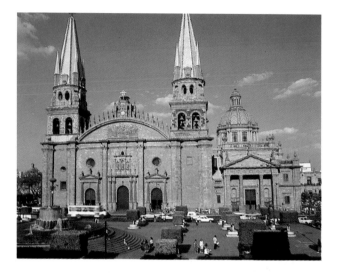

is on display at **El Museo de Orozco**, where he lived and had his studio.

Guadalajara's *Fiestas de Octobre* is a month-long celebration where international companies perform symphony concerts, opera and ballet. Other attractions include rodeos, bullfights, golf and tennis tournaments. **Zona Chapultepec**, with its centre walkway festooned with trees and fountains, boutiques, art galleries, haute cuisine restaurants, cafés and bookshops, is Guadalajara's own Zona Rosa.

WHAT TO SEE

◆◆◆
BARRANCA DE OBLATOS
11 miles (17km) along Calzada Independencia
A 2,000 foot (630m) canyon, that

Guadalajara can best be seen from the tall towers of the Cathedral

has been cut out in geological time by two rivers. A cable car descends to the canyon floor with its hot springs and lush vegetation.

◆◆
CATHEDRAL
Plaza de Los Laureles
The cathedral was started in 1571 and displays several styles of architecture, including Gothic, baroque and Renaissance. Note the *Assumption of the Virgin* by Murillo by the entrance to the sacristy.

◆◆◆
LAGO DE CHAPALA (LAKE CHAPALA)
One hour south of Guadalajara and popular for one day excursions, the lake was named after a Taltica Indian

chief. This is the largest lake in Mexico. On its shoreline is the pleasant resort of the same name. A popular meeting place is the Beer Garden at the end of the main street. Launches can be rented for a tour of the lake.

◆
MUSEO DEL ESTADO DE JALISCO (REGIONAL MUSEUM)
Next to the cathedral the museum has a large display of pre-Hispanic historic memorabilia.

◆◆◆
TEATRO DEGOLLADO
Plaza de la Liberacíon
Its vaulted ceiling is decorated on themes from Dante's *Divine Comedy*, and it has regular performances by the University of Guadalajara's folk ballet troupe as well as plays and concerts.

Accommodation

Moderate
The **Frances** is just off Plaza de la Liberacion, at Maestranza 35 (tel: 13-1190). It is the oldest hotel in Guadalajara, and is now a designated national monument. The rooms are pleasant – try to get one looking out on the Palacio de Gobierno – and there is a restaurant with live music and dancing. Rates are very reasonable.
The **Lafayette** at Avenida La Paz 2055 (tel: 30-1112), is in the

Using traditional methods, fish are still caught in the somewhat polluted water of Lake Chapala

heart of the financial district and close to the airport. Its 200 rooms have air conditioning, colour TVs and telephones. Prices are moderate and it is conveniently situated near the city's night clubs and best restaurants.

Others include:

Aranzazu (540 rooms) Revolucíon and Degollado (tel: 13-3232).

Calinda Roma (176 rooms) Juárez No 170 (tel: 14-8650).

Camino Real (210 rooms) Av Vallarta 5005 (tel: 21-7217).

De Los Reyes (171 rooms) Calzada Independencia Sur 164 (tel: 13-0076).

De Mendoza (110 rooms) V Carranza No 16 (tel: 13-4646).

Diana (180 rooms) Circunvalacíon Agustín Yanez 2760 (tel: 15-5516).

El Tapatío Resort and Racquet Club (207 rooms) Blvd Aeropuerto 4775 (tel: 35-6050).

Fiesta Americana (394 rooms) Aurelio Aceves 225 (tel: 25-3434).

Guadalajara Sheraton (222 rooms) Av Niños Héroes y de 16 Septiembre (tel: 14-7272).

Holiday Inn (305 rooms) López Mateos and Mariano Otero (tel: 31-5566).

Plaza del Sol (352 rooms) López Mateos Sur (tel: 21-4030).

Inexpensive

Canada (67 rooms) Dr Michel 218 (tel: 19-2092).

Chapalita (93 rooms) López Mateos 1617 (tel: 22-7710).

Colón (78 rooms) Ave Revolucíon Poniente No 12 (tel: 13-3753).

Colonial (24 rooms) López Mateos Sur 2405 (tel: 31-9101).

Continental (127 rooms) Corona 450 (tel: 14-1117).

Del Bosque (73 rooms) López Mateos 265 (tel: 21-4650).

Del Parque (77 rooms) Juárez 845 (tel: 25-2800).

Fenix (264 rooms) Corona 160 (tel: 14-5714).

Genova (63 rooms) Juárez 123 (tel: 13-7500).

Guadalajara (68 rooms) Vallarta 3305 (tel: 15-5725).

Internacional (112 rooms) Pedro Moreno 570 (tel: 13-0330).

La Estancia Del Sol (100 rooms) Mariano Otero 2407 (tel: 31-6164).

Las Pergolas (200 rooms) Morelos 2244 (tel: 30-1727).

Nueva Galicia (91 rooms) Corona 610 (tel: 14-8780).

Posada Guadalajara (170 rooms) López Mateos Sur 1280 (tel: 21-2022).

Posada Virreyes (60 rooms) On highway to Mexico City (tel: 35-6622).

Universo (137 rooms) López Cotilla 161 (tel: 13-2815).

Nightlife

Hotel Aranzazu, Bar Lafitte, Caballo, Negro, Buffalo Rock, Exelaris Hyatt Regency and Hotel Holiday Inn all offer lively evenings. Among the discos are **Osiris**, **Club Privado**, **Elipsis**, **Plantation**, **Genesis** and **Pip**. There is a very large range of restaurants to suit all budgets. Also many different kinds of cuisine – French at **Chez Pierre** and **Le Trianon**, German at **El Tirol**, Italian at **Trattoria de Giovanni**, Japanese at **Svehiro** and Mexican at **Brazz Campestre** and **Caporales**. This is just a short list from the many to choose from.

The beautiful bay of Acapulco is now fringed with high-rise hotels

RESORTS ON THE PACIFIC COAST

Of the three bodies of sea that surround Mexico, the Gulf, the Caribbean and the Pacific, apart from Cancún the most popular resorts are to be found on the Pacific. South from Mazatlán are 2,000 miles (3,218km) of spectacular and varied beaches. This area is in a state of continual development and improvement, although as the development of the coastline has moved in a southerly direction, you will find the more traditional resorts are along the northern shores. Set out below are some of the coastal playground venues which attract the visitor.

ACAPULCO

The luxury high-rise hotels which line 20 or more sun-drenched beaches and glittering Acapulco Bay attract the jet-set and holiday makers from all over the world. The centre of town, often referred to as 'traditional' Acapulco, lies on the western side of the Bay. The most popular beaches are in this area. **Playa Condesa** is the most frequented, but there are over 20 more, each fulfilling a different need (there are 'morning beaches', 'afternoon beaches', swimming and sporting beaches).
The Strip from the Exelaris Hyatt Regency to the Acapulco Paraiso is where the nightlife,

PACIFIC COAST RESORTS

The Acapulco Princess was designed to resemble an Aztec pyramid

restaurants and high class shops are to be found. On the mountain road, overlooking the surrounding bay, **Las Brisas**, with a host of villas, each with its own swimming pool, offers the privacy, luxury and service which has made it one of the most famous honeymoon complexes in the Americas. Along **Playa Revelcadero**, between the town centre and the airport, is the famous **Acapulco Princess**, built on the style of an ancient Mexican pyramid, and its sister hotel, the **Pierre Marqués**, originally built by Paul Getty as his own special hideaway. Both hotels feature golfing packages, with a choice of 18-hole championship courses.

Once Acapulco was the main port-of-call for ships laden with ivory, porcelain and silk from the Orient. Today, these have been replaced by visiting cruise ships and the *tianquis* or market place, has now become a major conference centre.

Hotels range from inexpensive to deluxe and among the leading international hotel chains with properties here are Hyatt, Sheraton Princess, Quality Inn and Stouffer Presidentes. Every kind of water sport is catered for along with tennis and golf. There are also a great variety of cruises, many with entertainment on board. Don't miss the high divers at **La Quebrada**. They dive at night time, by torchlight from a 135 foot (41m) escarpment into shallow rock pools.

Buses run regularly, virtually from one end of the Bay to the other, while an ocean-side promenade (*malecón*) edges the city's activity. West of the city, **Pie de la Cuesta**, is the best beach for watching Acapulco's spectacular sunsets.

WHAT TO SEE

◆◆
SAN DIEGO FORT
The 17th-century fort overlooks the cruise ship pier, and houses pre-Hispanic relics and other historical memorabilia pertaining to the State of Guerrero.

◆◆
LAGUNA DE COYUCA
West of the city, near the beach of Pie de la Cuesta
This is a freshwater lagoon and bird sanctuary enclaved by coconut palms, where you can swim or fish. The lagoon can be reached by canoe or rowboat, which can be hired at Pie de la Cuesta.

◆◆
CENTERO INTERNATIONAL
An amusement park for children featuring dolphin and seal shows, it also offers plays, symphony concerts and ballet during much of the year. Special performances can be seen on the billboard in front by the Costera.

Accommodation

Super Deluxe
The **Hyatt Regency** at Aportado Postal 565, Costera Miguel Alemán No 1 (tel: 4-2888), is located directly on Acapulco's Bay. It offers a pool shaded by palm trees and a variety of watersports at the beach.
Others include:
Acapulco Plaza (1,000 rooms) Aportado Postal C-88, Costera Miguel Alemán 123 (tel: 5-9050).
Acapulco Princess (1,031 rooms) Playa Revolcadera, Apartado Postal 1351 (tel: 4-3100).
Las Brisas (300 casitas) Aportado Postal 281, Carretera Escenica 5255 (tel: 4-1650)
Pierre Marqués (340 rooms) Playa Revolcadero, Apartado Postal 474 (tel: 4-2000).
Villa Vera Hotel and Racquet Club (100 villas) Aportado Postal 260 (tel: 4-0303)

Moderate
El Mirador at La Quebrada 74 (tel: 2-1111), is the place people come to watch Acapulco's famous cliff divers. The hotel has over 130 pleasant rooms with large bathrooms staggered at different levels along the hill and amenities include 3 pools and a night-club. Prices are moderate.
Others include:
Acapulco Ritz (278 rooms) Costera Miguel Alemán (tel: 5-7336).
Acapulco Tortuga (250 rooms) Costera Miguel Alemán 312 (tel: 4-8889).
Caleta (300 rooms) Caleta Beach (tel: 3-9940).
Calinda Acapulco Quality Inn (366 rooms) Costera Miguel Alemán 1260 (tel: 4-0410).
Copacabana (420 rooms) Tabachines 2 (tel: 4-3260).
Elcano (144 rooms) Av de las Palmas and del Parque (tel: 4-1950).
El Presidente (422 rooms) Aportado Postal 933, Costera Miguel Alemán (tel: 4-1700).

PACIFIC COAST RESORTS

El Tropicano (137 rooms) Costera Miguel Alemán 510 (tel: 4-1000).
Hyatt Continental (435 rooms) Aportado Postal 214, Costera Miguel Alemán (tel: 4-0909).
La Palapa (400 rooms) Fragata Yucatán 210 (tel: 4-5363).
Las Hamacas (125 rooms) Costera Miguel Alemán (tel: 2-6161).
Malibú (80 rooms) Costera Miguel Alemán 20 (tel: 4-1070).
Maralisa (90 rooms) Av Enrique el Esclavo (tel: 5-6677).
Maris (84 room) Costera Miguel Alemán (tel: 5-8440).

Inexpensive

Arbela (50 rooms) Costera Miguel Alemán 1270 (tel: 4-2164).
Autotel Ritz (103 rooms) Costera Miguel Alemán (tel: 5-8023).
Belmar (65 rooms) Gran Via Tropical (tel: 3-8098).
Casa Blanca (120 rooms) Cerro de la Pinzona (tel: 2-1212).
De Gante (143 rooms) Costera Miguel Alemán 265 (tel: 5-0232).
Los Flamingos (47 rooms) Av López Mateos (tel: 2-0696).
Mozimba (30 rooms) Playa Langosta (tel: 2-1529).
Vilia (60 rooms) Av Roqueta 154 (tel: 3-3311).
Also available are a plethora of reasonably priced self-catering condominiums and villas to rent.

Restaurants

Restaurants abound, offering everything from inexpensive local dishes to haute cuisine. Seafood is a speciality. Two good places to sample great seafood are **Beto's** on Condesa Beach (tel: 4-0473) with a very lively atmosphere and **Pipo's** just off the Costera (tel: 2-2237) where the food is excellent and very reasonably priced. There is also a big selection of discos, roof-top supper clubs with dancing and night clubs with shows.

Nightlife

In Acapulco the nightlife is world renowned. The choice of venues is so large and varied it is advisable to discuss the choice and prices with your hotel information desk.

IXTAPA/ZIHUATANEJO

By car, this relatively new, two-town, world class resort, is only 3½ hours drive from Acapulco and now has its own international airport. Once little more than the home of a few fisher folk, these scenic bays at the base of the Sierra Madre are popular venues for those who like to live less formally than in Acapulco. Considerable effort and care by the Mexican government has gone into opening up this area to visitors, while at the same time successfully retaining the natural beauty and unspoilt coastline. Sportsmen will enjoy a great variety of watersport, and there is an excellent golf course at the **Palma Real Golf and Tennis Club** in Ixtapa. One of the main attractions is nearby **Ixtapa Island**, which has a wildlife reserve and offers excellent snorkelling and diving. Fishermen will find in the waters around Zihuatanejo, just a few miles/km south of Ixtapa, an abundance of fish, including sailfish, marlin, roosterfish, yellowtail and bonito. Gear, bait and boats can be hired at the pier in Zihuatanejo. Boats also go out with parties who wish to snorkel and scuba dive, or there are moonlight cruises which can be booked in advance.

Accommodation

Super Deluxe
Camino Real (428 rooms, 6 suites) Palmar Bay (tel: 4-3330).
Club Méditerranée (375 rooms) Playa Quieta (tel: 4-2013).
Krystal (240 rooms) Palmar Bay (tel: 4-2618).

Moderate
The **Dorado Pacifico** situated at Palmar Bay (tel: 4-3060), is one of Ixtapa's nicest hotels. It has 285 pleasant, spacious rooms with balconies and amenities include a large pool with swim-up bar, tennis courts and parasailing.

Others include:
Aristos (226 rooms) Palmar Bay (tel: 4-2267).
Castel Palmar (110 rooms) Palmar Bay (tel: 4-2341).
Holiday Inn (238 rooms) Palmar Bay (tel: 4-2396).
Ixtapa Sheraton (381 rooms) Palmar Bay (tel: 4-3184).
Stouffer Presidente (440 rooms) Palmar Bay (tel: 4-2406).

Inexpensive
The **Sotavento** (tel: 4-2032) is located on the hillside above the beautiful white sands of La Ropa Beach. Its rooms are well-appointed – request one with a view of the sea – and French and international cuisine are offered at the two restaurants. Rates for the accommodation include breakfast and dinner.
Others include:
Playa Linda (250 rooms) Playa Quieta (tel: 4-3381).

Marvellous beaches in a sheltered bay are Zihuatanejo's hallmark

PACIFIC COAST RESORTS

MANZANILLO

Situated at the Costa de Oro, Manzanillo is a major port with excellent beaches, surrounded by jungle and fruit plantations; good for watersports and a centre for spectacular sea fishing. It lies about midway along the Mexican coastline, some nine hours drive northwest of Acapulco. An important annual deep-sea fishing tournament takes place in February. The port city is often referred to, in angling circles, as the sailfish capital of the world. Railway lines pass through the city to the docklands where freighters and naval ships tie up. Nearby, in the small harbour, fishing boats are for hire. Beyond the port, Manzanillo has many fine beaches where tourist accommodation is improving every year. **Playa Azul**, just around the bay, is a seven mile (11km) long beach lined with hotels, while the smaller **Playa Las Brisas** is a little further on. Sixty-one miles (98km) inland to the east is **Colima**, the provincial capital, with simple colonial buildings. Also in the region is the active volcano **Nevado de Colima**.

Accommodation

Accommodation is available to suit all pockets and the super deluxe **Las Hadas Hotel**, where Dudley Moore and Bo Derek frolicked in the film *10*, has its own yacht marina.

Super Deluxe

Las Hadas (206 rooms) (204 at Puerto Las Hadas nearby) Apartado Postal 158 (tel: 3-0000).

Moderate

Charles y Willie (40 rooms) 4m (6.5km) on route to Santiago (tel: 2-2906).
Club Maeva (514 rooms) Apartado Postal 442 (tel: 3-0595).
Club Santiago (300 rooms) Apartado Postal 374 (tel: 3-0413).
Condominios Playa Sol (120 rooms) Apartado Postal 414, Playa Azul (tel: 3-0309).
La Posada (24 rooms) Apartado Postal 135 (tel: 2-2404).
Roca del Mar (29 rooms) Playa Azul (tel: 2-0805).
Villas del Palmar (186 rooms) Apartado Postal 646, Playa Azul (tel: 3-0575).
Villas el Pueblito (52 villas) Av del Tesoro (tel: 3-0550).

Moderate

The **Colonial**, Avenida Mexico 100 (tel: 2-1080) in downtown Manzanillo is an unpretentious colonial-style hotel.
Also: **Las Brisas** (50 rooms) Av Cardenas (tel: 2-1951).

Economy

Savoy (24 rooms) Carillo Puerto 60 (tel: 2-0754).

Nightlife

Fairly limited in this area, but lively discos do exist, for example, at **La Cartouche** at Las Hadas, at the **Club Maeva**, the **Oasis** at Club Santiago and **Ostería Bugatti** by the Las Brisas intersection.

Restaurants

A good variety, ranging from places like **El Vaquero** which serves Hereford beef Monterrey style, to places with delicious seafood such as **El Camarón Despierto**.

PUERTO VALLARTA

Puerto Vallarta rests on Bahía de Banderas (the Bay of Banderas) some 175 miles (282km) north of Manzanillo. This bay is the largest natural bay in Mexico with many miles of coastline ringed by mountains. It was a sleepy fishing village until Richard Burton and Elizabeth Taylor made the film *Night of the Iguana* here in the 1960s. Since then this quaint town with its cobble-stoned streets, colonial-style street lighting, and pastel-coloured buildings, often decorated with bougainvillea, has become a popular seaside resort. Puerto Vallarta is now a modern resort offering a wide range of activities, which include waterskiing, windsurfing, sailing, parasailing, riding, tennis and golf. **Playa del Sol** is perhaps the most popular beach.

Twenty years ago Puerto Vallarta was only a sleepy fishing village!

Several large yachts provide half-day and full day cruises around the Bay, stopping off at the **Yelapa beach**, whose name means 'meeting place'. Between mid-May and early June is the main city fiesta with bullfights, *charredas* (rodeos), carnival floats and all manner of Mexican entertainment. A ferry service runs between Puerto Vallerta and **Cabo San Lucas** at the tip of Baja California: the crossing takes around 18 hours.

WHAT TO SEE

◆
ISLA RÍO CUALE
The Río (river) Cuale, picturesque in its upper stretches, separates into two arms just before passing into the sea. The river encircles an

PACIFIC COAST RESORTS

island in the centre of Puerta Vallarta, on which is a small museum, craft shops, open-air cafés and a children's playground.

A prime diving and snorkelling area is the sea around Los Arcos

◆◆

LOS ARCOS

To the south of town, Los Arcos are rock formations lying about 1,650 feet (500m) offshore, having been carved out by pounding waves. They can be seen from any southbound car, bus or boat.

Accommodation

Super Deluxe
Westin Camino Real (200 rooms) Hwy 200, Playa de las Estacas (tel: 2-0002).

Moderate
The recently renovated **Oro Verde** is centrally located at Rodolfo Gómez III (tel: 2-1555). Right on the beach, this Swiss-run hotel has over 160 pleasant rooms and suites and amenities include a swimming pool, restaurant and nightclub with dancing. Rates are moderate.
Others include:
Bougainvilias Sheraton (501 rooms/suites) ½ mile (1km) Tepic (tel: 2-3000).
Buenaventura (210 rooms) Av México No 1301, Cuale North (tel: 2-3737).
Castel Pelicanos (220 rooms) 1½ miles (2.5km) Tepic (tel: 2-2107).
El Lugar de Arturo and Pancho (307 rooms) 3 miles (5km) Tepic (tel: 2-2325).
Fiesta Americana (363 rooms) Playa Los Tules (tel: 2-2010).
Garza Blanca (22 suites/17 chalets/34 villas) 4½ miles (7.5km) Mismaloya (tel: 2-1023).
Holiday Inn Main Tower (230

rooms/6 suites) **Suite Tower**
(236 suites/10 penthouses) (tel:
2-1700).
Krystal Vallarta (500
rooms/suites/villas) three
miles (5km) Tepic
(tel: 2-1459).
Las Palmas (147 rooms) 1½
miles (2.5km) Tepic (tel:
2-0650).
Los Arcos (130 rooms/9 suites)
Olas Atlas, Cuale South (tel:
2-1583).
Molino de Agua (65 rooms)
Vallarta 130, Cuale South (tel:
2-1907).
Playa Conchas Chinas (32
suites/8 rooms/1 penthouse)
1½ miles (2.5km) Mismaloya
(tel: 2-0156).
Playa del Oro (400 rooms) 3½
miles (5.5km) Tepic (tel:
2-6868).
Plaza las Glorias (243 rooms)
Playa las Glorias (tel: 2-2224).
Plaza Vallarta (410 rooms)
Paseo de las Glorias (tel:
2-4360).

Inexpensive
Cuatro Vientos (13 rooms)
Matamoros No 520 (tel: 2-0161).
El Conquistador (108 rooms)
one mile (1.5km) Tepic
(tel: 2-2088).
Encino (75 rooms) Juárez 122,
Cuale North (tel: 2-0051).
Posada Roger (50 rooms)
Basilio Badillo Cuale North (tel:
2-0836).
Rosita (111 rooms) Díaz Ordaz
No 901 (tel: 2-1058).
Suites Las Garzas (11 rooms)
Av de las Garzas (tel: 2-1433).
Tropicana (249 rooms) Amapa
227, Cuale South (tel: 2-0829).

Economy
Marlyn (37 rooms) Mexico
1121, Cuale North (tel: 2-0965).

**Restaurants, Discos and
Night Clubs**
These are in such plentiful
supply that the visitor is spoilt
for choice.
El Viejo Vallarta, on Díaz
Ordaz, offers excellent
Mexican-style cooking, with a
particularly tasty *enchilada*,
while **El Dorado** on the beach,
is an ideal place to watch the
world go by.

MAZATLÁN

Mazatlán, or 'Place of the
Deer', lies on a rocky
promontory opposite the tip of
Baja California and has a ferry
service to **La Paz** on this
peninsula (crossing time, 16
hours). The nation's largest
shrimp fleet and the finest
harbour facilities of Mexico's
Pacific coast are found here.
Marlin and sailfish are caught
in great quantities year round
and eight fleets of charter
boats are on call to take
fishermen out. Situated on a
headland, there is a choice of
beaches, some have evocative
names; **Las Gaviiotas** (the
Seagulls), is the beach nearest
town, further north, **Playa
Sabalo** is the best of Mazatlán's
beaches while the island
beach of **Vendos** offers
exceptionally clear and calm
waters. The big rollers on
some of the beaches attract
surfing enthusiasts. Hunting for
everything from mountain lion
to wild boar is also available.
Every year three major events
take place here. The **Carnival**,
which some say is the best in
the world after Río de Janeiro
and New Orleans occurs

Surfing on huge Pacific rollers and sea fishing are popular in Mazatlán

between Friday and Tuesday before Lent. Accommodation for this event gets booked out six months in advance. The second is the opening of the fishing season when the Bishop of Mazatlán leads a procession down to the dock to bless the fleet. This takes place on 15 September. The third is the Mazatlán Fishing Tournament at the end of August, beginning of September.

After sundown, the palm-fringed and brightly-lit **Malecón** becomes a veritable ocean-side *paseo*, alive with strollers and passing vehicles of all descriptions, including four-wheel carriages, three-wheeled taxis and *arañas* (covered carts).

WHAT TO SEE

♦♦
EL FARO
Situated on **Cerro del Crestón**
the promontory separating the port from the ocean, is El Faro – one of the tallest lighthouses in the world.

♦♦
EL MIRADOR
Intersection of Paseo Claussen and Olas Altas
Once a lookout tower, now twice each day daredevil young divers plunge from the top into the sea below. Not as spectacular as the high diving in Acapulco, but dangerous nonetheless.

Accommodation

Moderate
The **Suites Las Flores** (122 units) at Loaiza 212 (tel: 3-5100), on the beach, is a high-rise hotel offering apartments with kitchens, ideal for a longer stay, as well as standard rooms. The atmosphere is easy-going and relaxed,

though its popular bar and beachfront can become very lively.
Others include:
Aqua Marina (101 rooms) Av del Mar 110 (tel: 1-7085).
Belmar (196 rooms) Olas Atlas Sur 166 (tel: 1-4299).
Camino Real (170 rooms) Punta del Sábalo (tel: 3-1111)
Caravelle Beach Club (125 rooms) Camarón Sábalo (tel: 3-0377).
Club Balboa (62 rooms) Camarón Sábalo (tel: 3-7784).
Costa de Oro (250 rooms) Camarón Sábalo (tel: 3-5344).
De Cima (200 rooms) Av del Mar (tel: 1-4119).
El Cid (1,000 rooms) Camarón Sábalo (tel: 3-3333).
El Dorado (41 rooms) Av del Mar 177 (tel: 1-4718).
Holiday Inn (200 rooms) Camarón Sábalo 696 (tel: 3-2222).
Hotel Tropicana (139 rooms) Loaiza 27 (tel: 3-8000).
Los Sábalos (185 rooms) Loaiza 100 (tel: 3-5409).
Oceano Palace (167 rooms) Camarón Sábalo (tel: 3-0666).
Playa Mazatlán (425 rooms) Loaiza 202 (tel: 3-4444).
Puesta Del Sol (72 rooms) Camarón Sábalo (tel: 3-5522).
Riviera Mazatlán (252 rooms) Camarón Sábalo 51 (tel: 3-4611).
Suites Las Sirenas (72 rooms) Av del Mar 1100 (tel: 3-1866).
Torres Mazatlán (60 rooms) Calzada Sábalo Cerritos (tel: 3-6330).
Yacht Club La Marina (103 rooms) Sábalo Cerritos (tel: 3-0222).

Inexpensive
Club Playa del Mar (61 rooms) Av del Mar 840 (tel: 2-0833).

Las Arenas (70 rooms) Av del mar 1910 (tel: 2-0000).
Posada Don Pelayo (100 rooms) Av del Mar 1111 (tel: 3-1888).
Suite Caribe Mazatlán (21 rooms) Av del Mar 1020 (tel: 3-1844).

Economy
Arlu (11 rooms) Albatros 2, Colónia Gaviotes (tel: 3-5212).

Restaurants
Specialising mainly in seafood and charcoal grilled steaks, and some have fancy names like **Senor Frog**, **El Shrimp Bucket** and **Los Pelicanos**. **Mamucas**, downtown at Simón Bolivar 73, is an exceptionally fine seafood restaurant.

Discos
Many of the numerous discos such as **Oh Baby**, **Tony's Plaza** and **Valentino's** are not so imaginatively named.

HUATULCO

The Bays of Huatulco are located on Mexico's Southern Pacific Coast 22 miles (35km) east of **Puerto Angel**, in the state of Oaxaca. It now has its own airport and is the government's biggest tourist project since Cancún. Nine beautiful sandy bays, each specialising in a particular activity will be developed in this scenically stunning environment. Already a Club Méditerranée and a Sheraton hotel are in operation, while Santa Cruz Huatulco, a coastal village, is being transformed into an 'authentic Mexican Village'. Huatulco is scheduled to become Mexico's leading seaside resort.

BAJA CALIFORNIA

Baja California, 782 miles (1,260km) in length, and mainly desert, is longer than the peninsula of Italy, and attracts visitors because of its sea fishing and watersport, around its 2,111 miles (3,400km) of coastline. In some of the resorts there is a good development of hotels and prices are reasonable.

Sightseeing includes visits to the ruins of some of the early Spanish missions at **San Ignacio** and **Mulegé** and to caves where there are Indian paintings of hunting scenes, whose history is little known, and whose origins not yet completely understood. Besides the main border towns of **Tijuana**, **Tecate** and **Mexicali** which are particularly popular with day visitors from

The Cathedral at San José del Cabo

A statue of an Indian at Tijuana

of Baja California that the
Mexican government has been
encouraging the development
of new resorts, such as **Loreto**
and **San José del Cabo**.
Recently, the largest striped
marlin weighing 919lbs (417kg)
was caught in these waters.
At the extreme tip of the
peninsula lies **Cabo San Lucas**,
an idyllic spot where the
waters of the Sea of Cortés and
the Pacific meet, and seals can
usually be seen disporting
themselves.

WHAT TO SEE

♦♦
PINTURAS RUPESTRES (CAVE PAINTINGS)
Carried out centuries prior to
the arrival of Europeans. Little
is known about them; they
bear hardly any resemblance
to other Mexican art forms.
Indian legend relates that they
are a product of a race of

the United States, there is a
one hour further drive via a
good toll road to the charming
port of **Ensenada**, and about 22
miles (35km) from here, **La
Bufadora**, a blow-hole that
periodically spouts sea-water.
La Paz, made famous by John
Steinbeck for its pearl divers,
is popular for game fishing,
which is so good off the coast

giants from the north. Difficult to reach, best departure points Loreto and Mulegé.

♦♦♦

SANTUARIO DE LA BALLENA GRIS (GRAY WHALE NATIONAL PARK)

Twenty miles (32km) from Guerrero Negro is where the visitor can see the sea mammals which have migrated from the icy waters of Alaska to Scammon's Lagoon to breed.

Accommodation

Loreto

Moderate

Stouffer Presidente (250 rooms) Nopolo Bay (tel: 3-0700)
Stouffer Presidente La Pinta (50 rooms) Fco 1 Madero s/n (tel: 3-0025).

Inexpensive

Hotel Misión de Loreto at Calle de la Playa 1 (tel: 3-0048), is situated east of the plaza, along the waterfront. The 52 rooms are comfortable, and some have good views of the Sea of Cortés. There is a swimming pool and two restaurants and you can arrange to go out on fishing trips through the hotel manager.
Also:
Oasis (37 rooms) Baja Calif, and López Mateo
(tel: 3-0211)

Restaurants

For some of the best food in Loreto, try **Caesar's Restaurant** (tel: 3-0203). Seafood and a wide variety of meat dishes are offered at reasonable prices.

Cabo San Lucas/San José del Cabo

Super Deluxe

The **Hacienda** in Cabo San Lucas (tel: 3-0122) resembles an old Spanish hacienda with fountains and tropical gardens. It is conveniently situated for watersports, and there is a choice of rooms available. Quite expensive, but definitely worth it for the comfort, if you have the means.
Others include:
Cabo San Lucas (101 rooms) Corrida Tur Cabo (tel: 3-0123).
Finisterra (63 rooms) Domicilio Con Ocido (tel: 3-0000).
Palmilla (71 rooms) San José del Cabo (no local phone).
Solmar (70 rooms) Cabo San Lucas (tel: 3-0022).
Twin Dolphin (58 rooms) near Cabo San Lucas (no local phone).

Moderate

Calinda Aquamarina (100 rooms) San José del Cabo (tel: 2-0239).
Calinda Cabo Baja (120 rooms) Near Cabo San Lucas (tel: 3-0044).
Castel Cabo (150 rooms) San José del Cabo (tel: 2-0155).

Restaurants

There are good restaurants and nightlife in both the border towns and resorts. Prices tend to be a little high in Cabo San Lucas, but there are several places offering good food at moderate prices. **El Rey Sol** serves great Mexican dishes, especially breakfasts. You can enjoy similar fare at **Restaurant Fisher** or at **Restaurant Diana** in San José del Cabo.

SOUTHERN MEXICO

South Mexico is used here to describe the states of Oaxaca, Chiapas, Tabasco and part of Veracruz, although the latter is more to the east of Mexico City. It is a fascinating region, mostly mountainous, with lush jungle forests in certain areas, and with a near tropical climate.

OAXACA

Some 300 miles (483km) southeast of Mexico City, Oaxaca is a delightful provincial city set in a temperate and fertile valley, and ringed by the inspiring range of the Sierra Madre del Sur. The city and environs are steeped in pre-Columbian and Colonial traditions, making it one of the most interesting and attractive regions in Mexico. Visitors can see the ancient city ruins of **Monte Albán**, **Yagul** and **Mitla**, between Monte Albán and Mitla is one of the largest living trees in the western hemisphere.

This is the home of the Zapotec and Mixtec Indians, and the considerable Indian population of the region gives rise to interesting markets and shops, which sell a dazzling array of hand embroidered clothes, rugs, jewellery, leather and silver at inexpensive prices. **San Bartolo Coyotepec** is famous for black pottery, **Teotitlán** for hand woven *serapes* and **Yalaga** for raw silk shawls. On the 'Night of the Radishes', 23 December, booths are set up in Oaxaca for the display and sale of

The interior of Santo Domingo, Oaxaca, is richly ornamented

sculpted radishes portraying amazing nativity scenes. Streets of houses in Oaxaca remain unchanged since the Colonial period, which, along with the churches of **Santo Domingo de Guzmán**, the **Basílica Menor de la Soledad**, the **Cathedral** and **San Juan de Díos**, reflect a golden age of architecture. Architecturally, one of the most interesting hotels in the whole of Mexico is the **Stouffer Presidente**, the renovated 16th-century convent of Santa Catalina. The church of **Santo Domingo**, dating from the 17th century, is one of Mexico's greatest treasures. Inside it is a riot of baroque ornamentation.

SOUTHERN MEXICO

WHAT TO SEE

◆◆
CASA Y MUSEO BENITO JUÁREZ (HOUSE AND MUSEUM OF BENITO JUÁREZ)
Calle García Vigil 609
To understand further the influence and contribution which the Mesoamerican people have and continue to make to Mexico and her history, visit the home of her most famous president, Benito Juárez, who was a full blooded Zapotec. His background, rising from poverty to the highest position in the land, is similar in many ways to Abraham Lincoln, of whom he was a contemporary. Some of the rooms appear as they did in the middle of the last century.

◆◆◆
MITLA
Twenty-eight miles (45km) east of Oaxaca
Mitla contains some of the most precious remains in Mexico: the Hall of Columns – palaces whose walls are covered in highly artistic Grecian-style ornamentation, and the Column of Life, which, when grasped, is claimed to tell you how long you have to live.

◆◆◆
MONTE ALBÁN
Nine miles (14.5km) from Oaxaca.
These ruins of a religious Zapotec and Mixtec town are unique. Positioned on a mountain top, they cover 15 square miles, (39 sq km) and include the main square, the ball-court, an observatory, numerous tombs which honeycomb the hilltop and carvings referred to as 'dancers' (believed to be records of medical conditions and deformities).

◆◆◆
MUSEO DEL ESTADO (STATE MUSEUM)
The museum is next to Santo Domingo Church and houses an incomparable collection of Zapotec and Mixtec gold, silver, jade and turquoise *objects d'art* and some of the most interesting relics found in a Mixtec tomb in Monte Albán. The workmanship is exquisite.

◆◆
YAGUL
About 21 miles (33km) from Oaxaca
The ruined Zapotec fortress city of Yagul is on top of a mountain and overlooks three levels of palaces, temples and the largest ball-court in the Oaxaca Valley. There is an excellent view of the valley from the top.

Accommodation

Moderate
Misión de los Angeles (155 rooms) Calzada Porfirio Díaz (tel: 5-1500).
San Felipe Misión (160 rooms) Jalisco 15 (tel: 5-0100).
Stouffer Presidente (91 rooms) No 300 5 de Mayo (tel: 6-0611).
Victoria (151 rooms) Pan American Highway (tel: 5-2633).

Inexpensive
Marqués del Valle (tel: 6-3474) is situated right on the plaza at Portal de Claveria. Some of its

The Palace of Six Patios on the large archaeological site at Yagul

95 pleasant rooms have splendid views over the square, and the restaurant serves a substantial breakfast. The **Plaza** at Trujano 112 (tel: 6-2200), is a pleasant, well-kept hotel. The rooms are comfortable and arranged round a courtyard on two levels. Service is good and there is plenty of information available on where to go and what to see. Rates are very reasonable.

Others include:

Antequera (29 rooms) Hidalgo No 807 (tel: 6-4020).
Calesa Real (77 rooms) García Vigil No 306 (tel: 6-5544).
Francia (80 rooms) 20 de Noviembre (tel: 6-4811).
Isabel (64 rooms) Murguia No 104 (tel: 6-4900).
Mesón del Angel (34 rooms)
Miña No 518 (tel: 6-6666).
Mesón del Rey (22 rooms) Trujano No 112 (tel: 6-2200).
Monte Albán (18 rooms) Alameda de León (tel: 6-2777).
Señorial (127 rooms) Portal de Flores (tel: 6-3933).
Virreyes (31 rooms) Morelos 1001 (tel: 6-5555).

Restaurants

One of Oaxaca's specialities is *mole Oaxaque*, a spicy, chocolate-based sauce used on pork and chicken. To sample this and other local cuisine try **El Asador Vasco** (tel: 6-9719). As well as good food, entertainment is laid on every night. **Tito's** (tel: 6-7379) is also worth a visit. Here the food is varied and very reasonably priced.

Early evening entertainment can be enjoyed several times a week around the Zócalo and some of the hotels, such as the

SOUTHERN MEXICO

Stouffer Presidente and the **Monte Albán** have regional folk dance entertainment. Evening dancing and discos also exist. On the whole nightlife in this provincial city is more sedate than swinging.

Tuxtla Gutiérrez

This is the capital of Chiapas and home of the *Marimba* bands which often provide evening entertainment at the hotels. The **zoo** on the south side of Tuxtla is well worth a visit. Placed on a hill, some of the walks are steep.

Accommodation

Moderate
The **Bonampak Tuxtla** (tel: 3-2050) west of town at Blvd Dominguez has 112 units of which 26 are bungalows. It is a comfortable, modern hotel with a pleasant cafeteria and restaurant, and there are closed circuit TV, film shows, pools and tennis courts.
Gran Hotel Humberto (tel: 2-2080) is situated west of the Zócalo at Avenida Central Poniente. It has 119 rooms with air conditioning and en suite showers. Amenities include a restaurant, bar, cafeteria and nightclub/cabaret. Very good value at a reasonable price. Also:
Real de Tuxtla (175 rooms) Carretera Pan-Am (tel: 2-5958).

Restaurants
Well worth a visit is **Las Pichanchas**, east of the Zócalo (tel: 2-5351) where you can get outstanding Mexican food in a charming setting at extremely moderate prices.

SAN CRISTÓBAL DE LAS CASAS

Seven thousand feet (2,134 metres) up in the Chiapas highlands, San Cristóbal is populated mainly by poor but very dignified Chamula and Zinacantecas Indians, usually dressed in colourful traditional costume. The name of the city honours Bartolomé de las Casas, who was the first Bishop of Chiapas. Take some warm clothing and an umbrella along, for it can be quite cold and wet in this area. San Cristóbal is the home of some of the finest Colonial architecture. Just north of the Zócalo lies the baroque church of **Santo Domingo** which is distinguished by its lovely pink façades. The former convent next door is the **Craftwares**

Museum, and local artefacts can be bought here.

WHAT TO SEE

◆◆
CASA NA BOLOM
Chiapa de Corzo
Former home of the Danish anthropologist, Frans Blom (lived in now by his widow), now a museum of local archaeology and ethnography, concentrating on the Lacandón Indians, the most remote and elusive of all Mexican tribes.

Accommodation
Comfortable but not luxurious; there is not much nightlife.

Inexpensive
El Molino de la Alborado at Aportado Postal 50 (tel: 8-0935), is close to the airport and easy to reach. All 11 rooms have an

attractive fireplace and there is a 9-hole golf course.

The **Posada Diego de Mazáriegos** (tel: 8-1825) is close to the Zócalo on Adelina Flores and is a delightful colonial-style hotel with 50 rooms.
Others include:
Bonampak (34 rooms) Calzada México (tel: 8-1621).
Español (36 rooms) Uno de Marzo (tel: 8-0045).
Palacio de Moctezuma (37 rooms) León and Juárez No 16 (tel: 8-0352).
Parador Ciudad Real (48 rooms) Diagonal Centenario (tel: 8-1886).
Parador Méxicanos (25 rooms) Cinco de Mayo (tel: 8-1515).
Rincón del Arco (21 rooms) Ejercito Nacional (tel: 8-1313).
Santa Clara (39 rooms) On the Zócalo (tel: 8-1140).

Restaurants
San Cristobal has a range of small restaurants to suit most tastes. **Restaurant Tuluc**, just up from the Zócalo (tel: 8-2090), is very popular. It offers a wide variety of dishes.

VILLAHERMOSA

Villahermosa, capital of the state of Tabasco, is an important industrial centre for the oil industry. There is a good selection of hotels in the area.

WHAT TO SEE

◆◆◆
PARQUE LA VENTA (VENTA PARK)
This park, set on the outskirts of the city, is an outdoor Olmec museum displaying altars and massive carved stone heads. a curious puzzle with their flattened, negroid features, in a setting like the one in which they were originally found. Deer, monkeys and anteaters wander freely while alligator and jaguars can also be seen. There is also boating on the **Laguna de Ilusiones** (Lagoon of Illusions).

Accommodation

Moderate
Cencalli (116 rooms) Paseo Juárez (tel: 2-6000).
Choco's (80 rooms) Constitucíon (tel: 2-9444).
Exelaris Hyatt (210 rooms) Juárez No 106 (tel: 3-4433).
Holiday Inn (276 rooms) Paseo Tabasco (tel: 3-4400).
Manzur (115 rooms) Madero No 422 (tel: 2-2499).
María Dolores (80 rooms) Aldama No 404 (tel: 2-2211).
Maya Tabasco (100 rooms) Av Grijalva (tel: 2-1111).
Miraflores (70 rooms) Reforma No 304 (tel: 2-0054).
Plaza Independencia (62 rooms) Independencía No 123 (tel: 2-1299).
Viva (260 rooms) Paseo Tabasco (tel: 2-5555).

Restaurants
The choice of food in Villahermosa reflects a Mayan influence.
Los Pepes, between Méndez and Zaragoza (tel: 2-0154) offers food which is based on tropical ingredients from the Yucatán. **Las Blancas Mariposas** serves decent sea food, but is closed on Mondays.

The Tomb of Inscriptions at Palenque is concealed in a nine-tier pyramid

PALENQUE

Although in Chiapas, this site is most easily reached by road from Villahermosa around 90 miles (145km) away to the northwest. In the jungle setting of Palenque lies a whole city, believed to have been the ceremonial centre of the great Mayan dynasty, which includes the **Templo de las Inscripciones** (Temple of Inscriptions) where the famous 'Man in the Jade Mask' tomb was found in 1946. Today, the visitor can climb the great stairway from the ground to the temple and then descend nearly as far down again to the burial chamber itself. Near by is the **Palace** complex and the **Templo de la Cruz Foliada (Temple of the Leafed Cross)** on a tiered pyramid. Its chamber, which was a sanctuary, has at the far end an altar covered by three linked panels of the cross. The cross, a stylised maize plant, was the symbol of life. The cooling waters of the **Cascada Motiepa**, a waterfall, are just down the road from the site's parking area. There is a selection of hotels.

To the southeast of Palenque, located deep in the jungle of Chiapas is **Bonampak**. Here you will find some of the finest Maya murals discovered so far. The site can be reached by charter plane from either Villahermosa or San Cristóbal.

VERACRUZ AND ENVIRONS

Veracruz was for centuries Mexico's major sea port. From

the docks, visitors can see the fortress of **San Juan de Ulúa**, built in 1582 to protect the port from pirates; later it became a notorious prison. In the heyday of Hollywood, many black and white films were made here. Veracruz is the home of the Latin American dance called the *bamba*. Marimba music remains a feature of evening entertainment around open air cafés.

Villa del Mar is the principal beach in Veracruz. Six miles (9.6km) out of the port, at **Mocambo**, is another fine beach bordered with pinewoods, and in a fishing village just beyond, called **Biza del Río** are good open air seafood restaurants overlooking the river.

Beaches on the **Isla Sacrificios** are reached by a launch trip. Excursions take the visitor to **Jalapa**, where there is a fine anthropological museum, to the Totonac ruins at **Zempoala**, and to **Tlacotalpan** where the wealthy hid from pirates.

WHAT TO SEE

◆◆◆
EL TAJÍN

The only major archaeological zone in the upper Gulf Coast region. Noteworthy ruins are the famous **Pyramid of the Niches** built by the Totonacs, the **Palace of Columns** and the great number of ball-courts.

◆◆
EL VOLADOR

A religious rite, sometimes referred to as the *Flying Indians*, takes place every Sunday in **Papantla**. This thrilling feat involves four Indians leaping off a tall pole to which they are tied, and spinning to the ground, while a fifth plays a pipe while perched on the top (see page 15).

Accommodation

Moderate

The **Emporio** (tel: 32-7520) with 200 rooms, overlooks the harbour at Paseo del Malécon. There are 3 pools, a roof garden, a disco and several cafeterias and restaurants. Others include:
Hostal de Cortés (100 rooms) Blvd de las Casas (tel: 32-0065). **Puerto Bello** (110 rooms) Avila Camacho (tel: 31-0011).

Inexpensive

The **Colonial** (tel: 32-0193) is situated right on the Zócalo at Miguel Lerdo 117. It is a well-maintained hotel with 180 rooms.
Others include:
Acuarío (80 rooms) Valencia (tel: 37-4573).
Real del Mar (69 rooms) Avila Camacho No 2707 (tel: 37-3634).

Restaurants and Nightlife

Seafood from the Gulf is the speciality in local restaurants.**Gran Café de la Parroquia** (tel: 32-2584) just off the Zócalo is a favourite meeting place. **La Paella** (tel: 32-0322) serves excellent fish. Leading hotels provide night entertainment and good downtown discos include **Capo's** and **Perro Salado** on the Avila Camacho Boulevard and **Plaza 44** on the Plaza de Armas.

The statue of Benito Juárez outside the Palacio Gobierno, Monterrey

NORTHERN MEXICO

Reaching from the Sea of Cortés, or Gulf of California, to the Gulf of Mexico, Northern Mexico is perhaps more of a business area than a holiday and resort region. With the exception of the coastal strips, the northwestern territory is for the most part plains, mountains and desert. The mountain ranges are rich in minerals. In other less harsh and difficult domains than the desert lie the grainfields with the coastal fringes being particularly rich farming country.

In northeastern Mexico is **Monterrey**, the industrial capital and third largest city with over two million inhabitants. Within this region a business traveller with limited time off would have a choice of visiting the largest cities, some of considerable architectural interest, of the five states in this area which include **Coahuila, Nuevo León, Tamaulipas, San Luis Potosí** and **Zacatecas**. For example, the latter, which derives its name from the Aztec words *zacatil* (grass) and *tlan* (place), is surrounded by the impressive mountains of Mexico's Sierra Madre Occidental, and successfully combines the roughness of its geographical terrain with the aristocratic flavour and elaborate architectural and colonial design of the buildings around the zócalo, thus symbolising the wealth that Zacatecas achieved in the 18th century, as one of the world's great silver mining centres. From a more tourist point of view there is one trip that is a great experience; it is on the **Ferrocarril de Chihuahua al Pacífico**, (Chihuahua Pacific

The Fuente de la Vida, *or Fountain of Life, is one of several in Monterrey's huge Gran Plaza*

Railway) 'the world's most scenic railroad' between **Chihuahua** and **Los Mochis**. Here the **Barranca del Cobre** (Copper Canyon) route cuts through a rugged section of northern Mexico's Sierra Madre. Four times larger and 280 feet (85m) deeper than the Grand Canyon, the train takes 12 hours one way, covering some 400 miles (640km) and passing through 86 tunnels and over 39 bridges, providing breathtaking views of spectacular mountain scenery. The line's highest point is **Los Ojitos** at 8,681 feet (2,646m). There are two major, de luxe, air-conditioned trains departing every morning, at 07.00hrs from both Los Mochis and Chihuahua, at opposite ends of the line. Reserved tickets can be purchased from both stations. To get the full benefit of the grandeur and beauty of the canyons, it is best to take the Los Mochis to Chihuahua route in order not to risk missing any of the magnificent scenery, as at certain times of the year it gets dark early.

Better still is to stay overnight en route at certain places such as **El Fuerte, Cuitéco, Cerocahui, Divisadero** and **Creel**. In some places, for instance Barranca del Divisadero, it is possible to ride on horseback along the edge of the canyons as well as to walk. At Creel you can visit the **Sierra Tarahumara**, home of the Tarahumara Indians, Mexico's most primitive and isolated tribe. Minibuses or jeeps are available to take you through the area.

THE YUCATÁN PENINSULA

The Yucatán Peninsula is the home of the Maya, one of the greatest civilisations ever known. It is studded with many fascinating archaeological sites and also encompasses the modern holiday playground of **Cancún**, on the edge of the Caribbean, which attracts a million visitors a year seeking sea, sand and sunshine.

MÉRIDA

Capital of the state of Yucatán and near the southern Caribbean coast, this colonial city, or 'White City' as it is known, was built in 1542, and straddles the site of the ancient ceremonial centre of Tiho, which was the last of the Maya strongholds to be defeated by the Spaniards. The Montejo family, who settled here afterwards, have a house, **Casa de Montejo**, dominated by a façade of bas-reliefs in the main square showing the arrogance of the Spanish knights standing on the heads of vanquished Maya. It is now a branch of the Banco Nacional de México.

On the opposite side is the **Ayuntamiento City Hall**, with its beautiful doorways and murals depicting the history of Yucatán. Other buildings in this very attractive Zócalo are the **Cathedral** and **Palacio de Gobierno**, now the headquarters of the State government. Before the advent of synthetic fibres, this city was rich from the export of sisal. Now, with its whitewashed walls, squares with fountains, flower-bedecked parks and relaxed way of life, it provides an ambience of faded gentility, which is very soothing. It remains one of the main departure points, along with Cancún, to the important Maya sites of **Uxmal**, **Chichén Itzá** and **Tulum**, and is a scheduled stop on most of the organised tours of this part of Mexico. Hotels cover the range, some being in attractive neo-classical style, some of an older vintage.

WHAT TO SEE

◆◆◆
CHICHÉN ITZÁ
75 miles (121km) east of Mérida
One of the biggest Maya archaeological sites in existence, it extends over six square miles (15.5 sq km). The huge ball-court, the size of a football pitch, is the largest that has been found. **El Castillo** or **Temple of Kukulkan** (Quetzalcoatl) is the centrepiece and is the result of a Maya-Toltec fusion. Note the **Temple of Warriors** with its snake-like columns and its Chacmol, a splendid reclining figure holding a vessel on which offerings to the gods were placed. Also, the **Cenote Sagrado** (Sacred Well) into which young girls, adorned in jewellery, were thrown as sacrifices to Chac, the god of rain.

◆◆
COBÁ
30 miles (48km) inland from Tulum
Recognised as probably the

biggest Maya site yet discovered and comparable in importance to Chichén Itzá, Cobá has a network of limestone-constructed, ceremonial roads, running over its 18 square miles (47 sq km). It has been totally reclaimed from the jungle and work began in the early 1970s to excavate it. The task will probably take half a century to complete properly.

◆◆◆
TULUM
70 miles (113km) south of Cancún

When the Spanish first saw this city in 1518 they remarked that it was as large as Seville. It is one of the few walled sites, with a pyramid called 'The Castle'. The attraction really is its setting, perched on the top of a high cliff overlooking the Caribbean.

◆◆◆
UXMAL
50 miles (80.5km) south of Mérida

A magnificent ruined Maya city with some of the finest proportioned and lavishly decorated buildings in Mesoamerica. Note in particular the oval **Pyramid of the Magician** in front of the beautifully laid out quadrangle of the **Nunnery**. After dark there is a spectacular sound and light show.

Accommodation

Moderate
Autel (106 rooms) Calle 59 (tel: 21-9175).
Calinda Pan Americana Quality Inn (110 rooms) Calle 59 (tel: 23-9111).
Casa del Balam (54 rooms)

Legend says Uxmal's Pyramid of the Magician was made in one night!

The Nunnery at Uxmal is decorated with carved friezes of Mayan huts

Calle 60 (tel: 24-8844).
El Castellano (170 rooms) Calle 57 (tel: 23-0100).
Holiday Inn (210 rooms) Colon at Montejo (tel: 25-6877).
María del Carmen (70 rooms) Calle 63 (tel: 23-9133).
Mérida Misión (148 rooms) Calle 60 (tel: 26-9667).
Montejo Palace (90 rooms) Montejo Blvd (tel: 21-1641).

Inexpensive
The **Caribe** (tel: 21-9232), once a convent, is now a small hacienda-style hotel on Calle 59, close to the Zócalo. Its 60 rooms are clean and comfortable and there is a small roof-top pool and a deck which overlooks the plaza. This is a very popular hotel and great value for money.

The **Posada Toledo** (tel: 23-2256) is not far from the plaza, at 487 Calle 58. This small colonial-style hotel has a magnificent garden and a roof deck which offers super views of the city. Not all the rooms are air conditioned but they are all tastefully furnished and well-kept. Rates are very reasonable.
Others include:
Alfonso García (80 rooms) Calle 86B (tel: 21-6496).
Aluxes (109 rooms) Calle 60 (tel: 24-2199).
Cayre (100 rooms) Calle 70 (tel: 21-1652).
Colón (54 rooms) Calle 62 (tel: 23-4355).
Colonial (52 rooms) Calle 62 (tel: 23-6444).
Del Gobernador (59 rooms) Calle 59 (tel: 21-3514).
Del Parque (21 rooms) Calle 60 (tel: 21-7840).

Dolores Alba (8 rooms) Calle 63 (tel: 21-3745).
Gran (36 rooms) Calle 60 (tel: 24-7622).
Paseo de Montejo (92 rooms) Montejo Blvd (tel: 23-9033).
Peninsular (49 rooms) Calle 58 (tel: 23-6902).
San Luís (40 rooms) Calle 61 (tel: 21-7580).
Sevilla (45 rooms) Calle 62 (tel: 21-5258).

Economy
Centenario (33 rooms) Calle 84 (tel: 23-2532).
Mucuy (10 rooms) Calle 57 (tel: 21-1037).

Restaurants
Mérida's specialities include meat and fish baked in banana leaves and a delicious *sopa de lima* (chicken in lime broth).
Los Almendros (tel: 21-2851) is a very popular place to sample the local cuisine, and though service can be slow, it is well worth the wait.

CANCÚN

Cancún has developed in the last two decades from a tiny fishing village of 115 people and a stretch of empty beach to a world-class playground with a year-round population of 70,000. Great credit is due to the foresight of the Mexican government, who saw the holiday potential in this area and encouraged development for tourism.
This Costa Brava of the Caribbean attracts visitors from all over the world, offering a resort holiday to suit all tastes and budgets. Cancún is actually an island – a thin stretch of sand connected to the mainland by two bridges. The city beach of **Playa Tortugas** is the centre of activities. It is also another departure point for tours to many interesting Maya sites. Cancún is also a port of call for cruise ships and a busy shopping centre. Besides visiting **Cozumel**, from here many visitors also take the ferries out from nearby **Puerto Juárez** or **Punta Sam** to the attractive little **Isla Mujeres**, where the Spaniards first set foot in what is present-day Mexico.

Accommodation
Supermarkets can provide for those who want to self-cater and hotels abound in every price range. Cancún and its environs has some forty to fifty hotels and below are listed those in the hotel zone on the Kalkulkan Boulevard.

Super Deluxe
Camino Real (281 rooms) (tel: 3-0100).
Hyatt Regency (300 rooms) (tel: 3-0966).
Krystal (325 rooms) (tel: 3-1133).
Sheraton (342 rooms and 132 suites)(tel: 3-1988).

Moderate
The **Casa Maya** (tel: 3-0555) is only three miles (5km) from the city. Its 350 rooms are large, with luxurious bathrooms. Amenities include three pools, tennis courts, moped rental and a restaurant. Very popular with families but a little expensive.
Others include:
Aristos (22 rooms) (tel: 3-0011).
Beach Club (165 rooms)

There are several deluxe hotels like the Hyatt Regency in Cancún

(tel:3-1177).
Calinda Quality Inn (280 rooms) (tel: 3-1600).
Castel Flamingo (90 rooms) (tel: 3-1544).
Club Lagoon (91 rooms) (tel: 3-0811).
Hyatt Caribe (202 rooms and 21 villas) (tel: 3-0044).
Misión Miramar (255 rooms and suites) (tel: 3-1755).
Playa Blanca (72 rooms) (tel: 3-0344).
Villas Plaza Cancún (636 rooms) (tel: 3-1022).
Viva (212 rooms) (tel: 3-0019).

Inexpensive
Caribe Mar (105 rooms) (tel: 3-0811).

Nightlife
Discos are as numerous as pebbles on a beach. Every night of the week there is a Mexican fiesta at one of the big hotels and for something different, try an evening 'pirate cruise' over to Isla Mujeres.

Restaurants
In Cancún restaurants are numerous and seafood is a speciality. **El Pescador** (tel: 4-2673) is probably the best place to get seafood in Cancún. Fresh lobster, red snapper and shrimps are served at a very reasonable price. **Los Alemandros** on Avenida Bonampak (tel: 4-0807) serves good traditional Yucatecan food, and is very cheap.

COZUMEL

The island of Cozumel is easily reached from the mainland by ferry, being just over a dozen miles (19km) offshore. It can be reached by hydrofoil or aircraft from Cancún, or by ferry from **Playa del Carmen** and **Puerto Morelos**. Cortés regrouped his fleet from Cuba here, before sailing to Veracruz to start his conquest of Mexico. The island is 30 miles (48km) long and nine miles (14.5km) wide and is a port of call for cruise ships. Duty-free shops line the waterfront of its main town, **San Miguel**. Visitors come from all over the Americas to scuba dive and snorkel – the **Chankanaah Lagoon**, south of Cozumel is the best spot. **Palancar**, off the southwest coast, is the second longest coral reef in the world, after Australia's Great Barrier Reef. It is now a national park and spear fishing is forbidden.

Accommodation

Moderate

La Ceiba (tel: 2-0379) is south of San Miguel on Paradise Point. It is a favourite place for scuba divers and has a beach which offers fine snorkelling. Other amenities on offer are tennis, a sauna, good restaurant, cocktail lounge and boat rentals can be made. Others include:
Cabañas del Caribe (bungalows, 56 on the beach) North Zone (tel: 2-0072).
Cantarell (100 rooms) North Zone (tel: 2-0144).
Club Cozumel Caribe (260 rooms) Playa San Juan (tel: 2-0288).
El Cozumelaño (80 rooms) Playa Punta Norte (tel: 2-0149).
Mara (50 rooms) North Zone (tel: 2-0300).
Mayan Plaza (94 rooms) Playa Santa Pilar (tel: 2-0627).
Playa Azul (40 rooms and 20 bungalows) Playa San Juan (tel: 2-0033).
Sol Caribe (220 rooms) South Zone (tel: 2-1711).
Stouffer Presidente (200 rooms) South Zone (tel: 2-0322).

Inexpensive

Barracuda (34 rooms) Av Rafael Melgar (tel: 2-0002).
La Perla (24 rooms) PO Box 309 (tel: 2-0188).
Maya Cozumel (30 rooms) Calle 7 Sur No 4 (tel: 2-0011).
Méson San Miguel (97 rooms) Av Juárez (tel: 2-0333).
Paraiso Caribe (37 rooms) Av Norte (tel: 2-0740).
Villablanca (20 rooms) Playa Paraiso (tel: 2-0730).
Vista del Mar Av Melgar (tel: 2-3333).

Restaurants and Nightlife

People dine early in Cozumel and most of the restaurants are in the town. They are somewhat overpriced by Mexican standards, but there is a good selection to choose from. **Pepe's Grill** (tel: 2-0213), along the waterfront, is an excellent place for seafood and steaks and is very moderately priced, while good Mexican snacks are served at **Plaza Leza** (tel: 2-1041), a sidewalk café situated on the main plaza. Waterfront discos include **Neptuno** and **Scaramouche** and keen scuba divers go out on night dives.

PEACE AND QUIET

Wildlife and Countryside in Mexico

by Paul Sterry

Geographically speaking, Mexico is an extremely varied country, even by Central American standards. It is dominated by a central mountainous plateau, which is flanked on either side by peaks, some of which rise to over 12,000 feet (3,600m). Volcanoes are frequent features, and the seismic activity of the Earth's crust also manifests itself in the occasional earthquake.

To the east of the mountains, the land drops steeply to the coastal fringes of the Caribbean and Gulf of Mexico, while to the west lies the Pacific Ocean. These coastal lowlands are markedly different in both vegetation

Beyond the scattered trees of the farmland are dense rainforests

and wildlife from the higher elevations inland. The Baja California and Yucatán peninsulas are also of interest; their comparative isolation has ensured many unique features.

Mexico City and the Central Highlands

With an expanding population, which some recent estimates claim to be fast approaching 15 million, Mexico City and the surrounding districts are unlikely destinations for the holiday naturalist. It is certainly true that, with the exception of a few hardy and tolerant species of bird, little wildlife interest remains within the boundaries of the metropolis. However, by making day excursions away from the hustle and bustle and choking air pollution, visitors can still find plenty to see around forested archaeological ruins and in national parks. Crime is a real threat to Mexico City's visitors, particularly those with such luxury items as cameras and binoculars. Exercise common sense when using these items, and try to make any excursions with a few like-minded companions.

Close to the centre of Mexico City lies Chapultepec Park, one of the largest and most popular urban recreational areas. Visitors from Europe may be somewhat intrigued to see introduced house sparrows flourishing alongside native birds such as Inca dove, house finch, canyon wren and American robin. Travel west towards Toluca along Highway 15 and you begin to ascend the hills and mountains which finally limit the city's expansion.

By turning south off Highway 15 at La Ventura you can reach the Desierto de los Leones National Park, an extensive area of comparatively unspoilt fir forest. Although it is some way from the city, solitary exploration is still not to be recommended, but visitors should still manage to see birds such as red warbler, Mexican chickadees, pygmy nuthatch and gray silky-flycatcher. Similar areas of forest can be found in the Valle de Bravo, 100 miles (160km) west of Mexico City, the Lagunas de Zempoala National Park, south of the city near Cuernavaca, and on the slopes of Volcan Itzaccíhuatl,

east of Mexico City.

To the northeast of Mexico City lies the famous pre-Columbian city of Teotihuacán, dominated by the Pyramids of the Sun and the Moon. The surrounding desert landscape is dotted with cottonwoods and agave cacti, and harbours lizards and birds such as vermilion flycatchers, turkey vultures, canyon wrens and curve-billed thrashers.

Northern Central Mexico

Northern Central Mexico is the Mexico of the movies. This upland plateau is a land of arid plains, deserts and mountains which stretch from the USA border south as far as San Luís Potosí and Guadalajara. Modern agriculture may have changed the face of parts of the landscape, with arable fields replacing the natural thorn scrub, but vast areas of desert still remain. In addition, there are pockets of marshland and pools as well as forest-clad mountain slopes to add to the diversity of the wildlife and scenery.

More than any other country in Central or South America, Mexico is a land of cacti. Indeed, few serious cactus enthusiasts fail to tour the country at least once in their lifetimes. Several larger species, such as the prickly pear, have been exported to other parts of the world, but America is their native home with the northern, central highlands holding perhaps the greatest diversity of all Mexico's regions. Cacti come in all shapes and sizes, from

PEACE AND QUIET

small, compact cushions to the giant 'organ pipes' of the saguaro. What they all have in common is an ability to store water in times of drought, an essential quality considering Mexico's arid climate.

Associated with cactus vegetation is an extraordinary range of desert animals, each adapted in its own way to the rigours of the environment. Some use the cacti in a variety of unusual ways: woodpecker's excavate nest holes which later may be taken over by elf owls, and roadrunners nest among the dense spines for protection.

Many of the desert creatures are active only at night, hiding

A cardon cactus forest flourishes in Baja California's arid climate

in burrows or under boulders during the heat of the day. Rattlesnakes are well-known desert residents, but there are also lizards, ranging from tiny species to the large gila monster, and feeding on insects such as beetles. Scorpions also come out at night to feed on insects and other small prey.

After dark, desert rodents such as kangaroo rats are sometimes seen in car headlights and many are taken by predators such as coyotes and great horned owls. Most of the desert's other birds are diurnal and frequently encountered species include curve-billed thrashers, cactus wrens, brown towhees, turkey vultures, American kestrels, Inca doves and mourning doves.

PEACE AND QUIET

Yucatán

The Yucatán peninsula harbours a surprising range of habitats, some of which are rather uncharacteristic of Mexico as a whole. Although bordered to the southwest by a belt of tropical rainforest, much of Yucatán is far too dry for this habitat. Dry tropical forest gradually disappears towards the end of the peninsula, where arid thorn and cactus scrub predominate. Yucatán is justly famous for its Mayan ruins, but for the naturalist it is the coasts which are the highlight. Sandy beaches, rocky outcrops, coral reefs and mangrove-lined estuaries support a host of birds, mammals and reptiles. The ruins of Chichén Itzá and Uxmal are the best preserved and most accessible of Yucatán's Mayan remains. Both are surrounded by tropical forests, which are full

A fork-tailed flycatcher

of wildlife and well worth exploring. Iguanas, social flycatchers, ruddy ground-doves and groove-billed anis might all be seen in the ruins, while ocelots, coatimundis, spider monkeys, armadillos and iguanas and forest birds such as plain chachalacas, Yucatán jays, turquoise-browed motmots and masked tityras can be found in the surrounding jungle.

Mérida, the capital city of Yucatán state, is a good base from which to explore the northern coast. The channels of the Río Lagartos and the nearby saltworks lure thousands of greater flamingos, as well as several species of herons and egrets, plus brown pelicans, magnificent frigatebirds, laughing gulls and numerous migrant waders. Alligators and manatees, although scarce, still occur.

The Ría Celestún National Wildlife Refuge, to the west of Mérida, is an excellent destination and can be explored by boat. Flamingos spend the winter here and great egrets, snowy egrets, green backed herons, roseate spoonbills, neotropic cormorants, belted kingfishers, turkey vultures and numerous waders can be found all year. On the east coast of Yucatán, Isla Cozumel, Isla Mujeres and Isla Contoy are worth a visit for the marine life, birds and archaeological remains.

Palenque, Chiapas

Palenque, in the southeastern state of Chiapas, is one of the most famous and best preserved archaeological sites in Mexico. Dominated by its famous pyramid, in Mayan times Palenque was an important city set in the heart of the jungle. Today it is still surrounded by tropical rainforests, and this fascinating habitat provides both a wonderful contrast to the ruins and superb opportunities for wildlife enthusiasts.

Rainforests, particularly areas as extensive as at Palenque, are an unusual sight in Mexico. This is partly due to man's influence and partly because most of the country's climate is too dry to support this habitat. However, in this region of Chiapas, visitors can find steamy jungles with trees laden with bromeliads, orchids and other epiphytes, vines and creepers as well as beautiful waterfalls and species of birds and mammals not found in other regions of Mexico.

The forests are full of insects: cicadas call from high in the trees and butterflies fly along glades and paths.

Around the ruins themselves and the forest edge, birdwatching is somewhat easier than in the jungle itself. Black vultures, roadside hawks and black hawk-eagles occasionally soar overhead, while boat-tailed grackles, groove-billed anis, rufous-tailed hummingbirds, great kiskadees, brown jays and clay-coloured thrushes can be found.

Within the forest, observing wildlife can be rather frustrating at first. The high,

Countless butterflies are found in the forest around Palenque

dense leaf canopy, low light levels and shy nature of some of the birds and mammals can prove a challenge. Before long, however, visitors learn to follow sounds and movements and the creatures reveal themselves. Armadillos and coatimundis feed on the forest floor and share this habitat with little tinamous and ruddy quail-doves, and howler monkeys scream from the treetops. Hummingbirds with delightful names such as purple-crowned fairy and white-bellied emerald often come to investigate intruders, but such exotically-named birds as violaceous trogons, keel-billed toucans, blue honeycreepers, rufous pihas and lovely cotingas do not invite attention.

Catemaco

Catemaco lies about 105 miles (170km) southeast of Veracruz

PEACE AND QUIET

along Highway 180 close to San Andrés Tuxtla. The town is on the western shores of Lago Catemaco and wetland wildlife can easily be seen. Catemaco also lies within easy reach of a wide variety of other habitats, and this helps boost the range of species that can be encountered. There are patches of lush tropical rainforest plus beaches and estuaries on the nearby Gulf. Lake Catemaco is an immense body of water which can be explored both from its margins and by boat. Rich fish populations support large numbers of birds: neotropic cormorants, pied-billed grebes and least grebes frequent the open water, while snowy egrets, cattle egrets, little blue herons and great blue herons stalk along the shores. Several species of kingfisher also occur and these include belted, ringed, Amazon and pygmy kingfishers.

Open farmland and roadside verges are good for squirrel cuckoos, groove-billed anis, rufous-tailed humming birds, great kiskadees, social flycatchers, brown jays, clay-coloured thrushes and Montezuma oropendalas. This latter species nests in colonies, weaving large, flask-shaped nests suspended from the branches of trees.

As you travel further away from the town, patches of rainforest appear. The road which leads to the Estacion Los Tuxtlas Veracruz, north of Sontecompan, is a particularly good area, and trees festooned with epiphytic plants, vines

Great blue herons are among the many birds living on Lake Catemaco

and creepers can be seen. This is a public road, but the research reserve belongs to the Instituto de Biologia, Universidad Nacional Autónoma de México. Birds such as masked tityras, red-legged honeycreepers, blue-gray tanagers and hummingbirds such as violet sabrewings, fork-tailed emeralds and long-tailed hermits can be expected. The shores of the Gulf of Mexico make a contrast to the rainforests. Some of the beaches are good for shells, and the estuaries and mangroves harbour spotted sandpipers, grey plovers, semi-palmated plovers, laughing gulls, royal terns and magnificent frigatebirds.

Villahermosa

Villahermosa is a bustling city in the state of Tabasco in southeast Mexico. Parks and gardens within the boundaries of the city contain a surprising number of birds, but it is the surrounding countryside which offers the best opportunities for the birdwatcher. Cattle ranching has created large areas of open land and, together with the natural marshes and wetlands of the region, the open country birds can be seen extremely well. By driving the back roads to the south and east of Villahermosa, visitors will soon find fields, ditches or wetland areas full of wildlife. Almost anywhere is likely to be good, but for the best birdwatching opportunities be sure to visit the Usumacinta Marshes, a huge area of wetland to the east of the road to Frontera, and the wetlands to the south of the city around Jalapa. Along the roadsides, double-striped thick-knees feed unobtrusively in the fields and bright green lizards sunbathe on tree trunks. Birds such as scissor-tailed flycatchers, fork-tailed flycatchers, great kiskadees, boat-tailed grackles and groove-billed anis can be seen perched on fence posts or in branches. The area is particularly good for birds of prey, and species such as laughing falcons, roadside hawks, black vultures, turkey vultures, yellow-headed vultures, Aplomado falcons and white-tailed hawks are quite regularly seen.

One of the more unusual raptors of Usumacinta is the snail kite, which feeds almost exclusively on the large, amphibious apple snails found in the marshes. The kite's specially adapted hooked beak enables it to extract the snail's body from its shell. Piles of the broken remains can be found beneath favourite feeding perches.

The wetlands host a wide range of species which are widespread throughout Central America. Typical birds include neotropic cormorants, which perch in groups to dry their feathers, anhingas, white and brown pelicans, roseate spoonbills, wood storks, great egrets, snowy egrets and limpkins and black-bellied tree-ducks. Jacanas delicately pick their way across the marsh vegetation on incredibly long toes, and lucky visitors may even see a beautifully marked pinnated bittern or ringed kingfisher perched on a branch overhanging the water.

Green lizards are seen frequently

PEACE AND QUIET

Mexico's Atlantic Coast

Mexico's eastern coast faces on to the Gulf of Mexico, which is contiguous with the Atlantic Ocean. The land is varied both in appearance and vegetation, being influenced by the climate, the altitude and by man. On the coastal plain, open grassland areas cleared for cattle ranching and agriculture contrast with dense forests, while on the coast itself sandy beaches, mangroves and lagoons can be found. Inland, the lowlands soon give way to hills and mountains, which provide both relief from the heat and contrasting wildlife. Many beaches are good for shells, although their distribution on the sand is often curiously localised. In common with most popular coastal areas of the world these days, beaches near to resorts are generally scoured regularly, so you may have to travel farther afield for the best results. Beaches and mudflats on Mexico's Atlantic coast are also good for birdwatchers: willets, egrets, magnificent frigatebirds, brown pelicans and royal terns are regularly seen. Brown pelicans catch fish by plunge-diving into the sea for fish while the frigatebirds attack other seabirds, forcing them to disgorge their last meal.

The shallow, coastal waters are rich feeding and breeding grounds for fish and all sorts of other marine animals. A whole new world is revealed with the use of snorkel and mask. Colourful starfishes, sea urchins, sea fans, manta rays, parrotfish and bass are among the delights that await the visitor.

The proximity of the ocean moderates extremes in temperature and the summer rainfall encourages the growth of dense forest. The rainfall becomes heavier, and its effect more profound, the further south along the coast you travel, and in some areas the jungles resemble true tropical rainforests. In this terrain, armadillos and tinamous forage among the fallen leaves, and motmots, hummingbirds, trogons and woodpeckers haunt the higher canopy.

Further inland, as you move up the slopes of the Sierra Madre, pockets of cloud forest still remain. Here the trees appear stunted, seemingly weighed down by astonishing growths of creepers and epiphytic orchids and bromeliads.

Mexico's Pacific Coast

The Pacific coast runs from the Arizona border south to Guatemala and harbours some of the country's major holiday destinations. For the visitor with an interest in natural history, the region offers the best of both worlds, a wonderful climate and beautiful beaches, and coastal lagoons, mangroves and lush jungles. Holiday visitors to coastal resorts need not necessarily restrict themselves to lowland habitats; the foothills of the Sierra Madre shadow the coast for much of its length and offer widely differing wildlife.

FOOD AND DRINK

Food

The most common mis-conception about Mexican food is that it is mostly composed of chillies and is so hot that it will blow the top off your head! It is true that the chilli figures prominently but there are 200 varieties of chilli, ranging from mild to the very hot. In fact, there is only really one exceptionally hot chilli which is used in the Yucatán and was popular among the Maya. This is the *habanero*, which the Mayans called 'the crying tongue'.

Maize, or 'Indian Corn' or Sweetcorn is probably the most widely used ingredient in Mexican cooking followed by the chilli and then the tomato and avocado.

Part of the fascination of Mexican cooking is that it has drawn its influences from so many and varied sources over hundreds of years and represents a wide combination of Indian, European and American tastes. To the Aztecs we are indebted for chocolate, vanilla, potatoes, maize, pumpkins, squash marrows and mangoes as well as a cornucopia of other fruits, nuts and seeds.

The Spanish conquistadores brought beef and dairy products to Mexico as well as chickens, goats, pork, wheat, oils, sugar, olives, garlic, and a knowledge of viticulture as well as the vines themselves. They also introduced apples, oranges, pears, peaches and melons. Hence, it is not surprising that the cuisine of Mexico is highly developed and that different parts of this huge country have also developed their own style.

In Baja California, seafood figures prominently, especially in delicious seafood soups. Lobster, abalone (an edible mollusc with an ear-shaped shell) crabmeat, turtle steak and quail are served all along the Pacific Coast. Here haddock, clams, oysters, lobster and palm hearts, stuffed snapper fish, shrimp often cooked in a batter of beer, charcoal-grilled seafood and suckling pig are popular and readily available. Another favourite dish is *ceviche*, uncooked seafood marinated in natural lime juice.

In the northern states of Mexico, local favourites include steak, spare ribs and kid grilled over a fire of mesquite, and beef, lamb and bacon skewered together, usually served on a bed of rice.

In Guadalajara the visitor will find a dish of shredded beef or chicken mixed with tomatoes and onions and grilled, a popular choice.

The kitchen of the Convent of Santa Rosa in Puebla, now the Museo de Artesanias is the place where the sauce known as *mole poblano* evolved. I say evolved rather than created as no one chef could have suddenly decided to concoct a sauce of over 60 ingredients including chocolate, chillies, ground nuts, various fruits and some 30 spices. Turkey served in this sauce is now considered

FOOD AND DRINK

Guacamole *made with avocados, served with* tacos, *small corn pancakes*

a national dish and, incidentally, the sauce has a very subtle flavour, not at all sweet. It can also be served with chicken and *enchiladas*. In Oaxaca you will find *mole* offered with *tamales*. Oaxaca's *mole* is much darker in colour and milder in taste than that of Puebla. *Tamales* are generally made from steamed corn dough wrapped in a dry corn husk or a banana leaf. The *tamales* are usually filled with meat, vegetables, or chilli beans. Some are quite solid and are eaten like bread and the large ones have excellent filling qualities for hungry travellers.

In Chiapas, they make a delicious cheese, shaped like a cannon-ball. It is eaten plain or with a spicy meat filling. Yucatán is recognised for its fragrant and delicately flavoured dishes. The juice of sour Seville oranges mixed with garlic and black pepper is used for seasoning. Specialities include *tortilla* dipped in pumpkin seed sauce and filled with crumpled hard-boiled egg, suckling pig wrapped in a banana leaf and baked slowly, baby shark and Moro crab. The great variety of coconut dishes and the famous almond cake are popular with the visitor. Lime soup and the liberal use of lime juice helps to combat bacteria and can help to avoid upset tummies frequently referred to by Americans as 'Moctezuma's Revenge'.

In Veracruz, the red snapper fish, *huacinango*, is famous and so is the *plato jarocho*. Although the ubiquitous Tex-Mex food abounds throughout the country it will be clear by now that there is more to be enjoyed in the way of Mexican food.

Meals at the Mexican restaurants mentioned compare favourably in price with similar European or American establishments but not if the visitor orders imported wine, spirits or liquors, all of which are heavily taxed.

Drink

In the last ten years Mexican wine has improved in quality and is worth trying. The names to look out for are *Domecq*, *Santo Tomas* and *Hidalgo*. Mexican beer is very good and goes down well with the Mexican dishes. *Negra Modelo*, *León Negra* and *Nochebuena* are popular brands. The powerful *tequila*, distilled from the maguey cactus is the best-known Mexican spirit – it can be drunk straight with salt and lemon or mixed into a cocktail. The country's best mineral water comes from Hacienda Spa Penafiel.

Mexico has an excellent variety of non-alcoholic drinks and the exceptional quantity and quality of fruit available in Mexico, gives rise to a huge range of delicious drinks. These are easy on the pocket and quite likely to wean adults and children away from the ubiquitous manufactured beverages. *Horchata*, a sweet melon-seed drink is traditional. Many fruit juice bars are found throughout the country.

If you don't like sugar in your coffee you must be specific

about this. As a general rule coffee (*café*) is drunk sweet, and many restaurants buy their coffee with the sugar already added (*café de olla*). Instant coffee is readily available, and the decision regarding sugar can be your own. Indian or China tea (*té*) is not readily available, but it is worth trying *té de manzanilla* (camomile tea), and *verba buena* (mint tea). Incidentally, coconut milk tastes delicious and is an excellent antidote if you are suffering from 'holiday tummy'.

Glossary

Mexican dishes you are most likely to come across:

ate: a jellied paste usually made from guava or quince.

cabrito: boiled goat – mainly found in northern Mexico.

cajeta: usually made from goat's milk which is caramelised.

carnitas: chunks of pork, deep fried.

ceviche: a seafood cocktail of uncooked, marinated seafood with chopped onion, tomato, pepper, oil and avocado.

chilaquiles: fried *tortilla* chips with sauce and cheese.

chillies rellenos: peppers stuffed with cheese and minced meat, fried in batter and served in hot tomato sauce.

chongos: curdled milk, mixed with egg, syrup and cinnamon.

chorrizo: spicy sausage.

cochinita pibil: a Yucatán speciality – suckling pig cooked in banana leaves.

enchilada: this is a fried, flat cake of corn meal (*tortilla*) containing various fillings such as meat, fish, cheese.

guacamole: pulped avocado flesh mixed with onions, tomatoes, chillies and yoghurt. Used as a dip with *tacos* or as a side salad.

mixiote: mutton cooked in the skin of maguey spikes, in corn husks or banana leaves and served with a spice sauce.

picadillo: filling of minced meat, mixed with tomato and onion with various seasonings.

pozole: a very highly seasoned soup, including hominy (maize) kernels, chick peas, pork, radishes, sausage, tomato and whatever else the cook has to hand!

quesadilla: various ingredients fried inside *tortilla* dough, such as cheese and strips of chilli, meat or mashed potato squash flower.

taco: a taco is a *tortilla* (see below) wrapped around various ingredients and then fried.

tamales: steamed corn dough stuffed with pork or chicken and chilli sauces, wrapped in a dry corn husk or a banana leaf. They can also have a sweet filling.

torta: a sandwich made with French bread. It will be filled with either ham, chicken, cheese, beans or pork and will almost certainly contain some chillies.

tortilla: the versatile and ubiquitous *tortilla* is the staff of life in Mexico. It has many variations but in its basic form it is a thin cake of corn meal (wheat meal is used in the north). It is served with meals, spread with sauces and rolled up to hold various fillings.

SHOPPING

Unless you are very strong minded indeed you must prepare to be carried away by the shopping possibilities of Mexico, either in the *tianguis* (native market) or the boutiques in the many resorts. The visitor will find that there are two kinds of market. The permanent markets attract people from towns and villages round about and take place on one or two days each week. The markets of Oaxaca, Guadalajara and Acapulco are among the best.

The temporary markets are found in small towns and rural areas and on the outskirts of large cities and even at major crossroads. They are particularly lively and worth visiting during the holiday seasons around Christmas and Easter and on the special fiesta days.

Arts and Crafts

As with its cuisine, Mexico, with its arts and crafts, has many indigenous traditions and has also developed and made its own many external influences and traditions. Ceramic ware of every kind abounds throughout the country. It was well established when the Spaniards arrived. Until that time, the pottery was single fired at a low temperature in open fires and this pottery can still be found and is the least expensive. Single-fired, unglazed pottery is not safe to use for cooking or food because the pottery contains lead salts which will activate with certain foods and become poisonous.

The Spaniards introduced the potter's wheel, the enclosed kiln and lead glazes to Mexico. High firing kiln temperatures now make ceramics more durable. Majolica is the finest and consequently the most expensive pottery. The skill of making it was introduced into Puebla in the 16th century. The authentic majolica is decorated with Arab heraldic motifs of shields, lions and eagles. However, the potters of the Metepec, inspired by the straightforward candlestick introduced by the Spaniards, developed this into what is known as the Tree of Life design, adorned with birds and flowers (sometimes standing ten feet high). There is also (although not for the faint-hearted) the Tree of Death, which takes the form of a skeleton with branches decorated with skulls.

In the state of Michoacán, especially near Pátzcuaro, the visitor will find attractive dishes in 'earth' colours of browns and greens. In San Bartolo Coyotepec, near Oaxaca, families produce interesting black pottery. Distinctive red glassware is found in Guadalajara, especially in Tlaquepue where the glass blowing can also be seen, and crystal in Monterrey.

Weaving is the second most important craft in Mexico, and Oaxaca is the area renowned for the production of magnificent woollen blankets and rugs. The natural dyes are more expensive than commercial ones but far more beautiful. In Teotitlán del Valle rugs are woven to your own specifications. In Michoacán blankets and rugs are of simple design and soft natural colours but with a looser weave. Fine *serapes*, a fashion 'item' in Europe are also available in Saltillo. The *rebozo*, which can be either a shawl or stole, is made of wool or in some cases, silk. Very fine ones will pass through a finger ring and San Luís Potosí is especially famous for them. In Tlaxcala, the cheerful striped Saltillo spread is woven.

The Huichol Indians make yarn paintings which are constructed on a base of plywood and covered with beeswax. They then press acrylic yarn into the base to form a picture, usually on a mythological theme. The pictures were originally made as offerings for the gods. Yucatán is famous for its hammocks, and Mérida has the widest selection. You can choose from a variety of materials, ranging from twine, which is the cheapest, to luxuriously comfortable linen. There is a wide variety of traditional clothing, much of it elaborately embroidered with designs from different regions. The Oaxaca wedding dress is one of the most attractive and popular.

Tijuana is the place to buy all kinds of leather goods. The further south you go the more you will pay. Leather goods are also available in León (famous for boots and shoes), Guadalajara, Jalisco and Guanajuato, Oaxaca and Chiapas.

Mexico is the world's largest producer of silver and the Mexicans are very skilled in working it and other metals into lovely jewellery. Some of the best jewellery and other silver items are found in Taxco, Guadalajara and Mexico City. In Oaxaca you will find exquisite reproductions of pre-Columbian jewellery in gold and silver, as well as fine gold filigree work. Michoacán is famous for its copperware, best found in Pátzcuaro market and government craft stores. Bark paper paintings are sold throughout the country and you will find the greatest variety and best quality comes from the state of Guerrero.

Collectors of religious art are well served, with many artists creating *retablos* (primitive religious paintings on tin) and *milagros* (miracles) which are tiny religious amulets made of silver shaped like hearts or limbs and *santos* (wooden carvings of saints).

In Uruapán, the craftsmen are renowned for their lacquered chests, boxes and furniture made of hardwood. *Equipales* furniture, traditionally made of pigskin and wood, is found in the state of Jalisco.

Mexicans also make beautiful toys. They are charming and imaginative, reflecting the Mexican's love of children. Toys include puppets, snakes hiding in matchboxes, tops and rag dolls.

Fonart is the name of a chain of government shops throughout the country which offer a wide variety of typical art and craft products at set prices. You don't have to haggle here but their prices may be slightly higher than average although the quality will be good. A visit will give you an idea of what is potentially available elsewhere.

ACCOMMODATION

Mexico offers a wide range of accommodation from ultra modern and elegant hotels to more modest establishments known as *casas de huespedes* (guesthouses). Room prices in all Mexican hotels are controlled by the Secretaría de Turismo (Ministry of Tourism) and there is a five-star rating system, similar to that in Europe, with a wide price range between one and five star. When booking you should bear in mind that most accommodation rates are just that – they do not include meals. The cheaper hotels rarely provide a private bathroom but in only slightly more expensive ones there may be the option to pay an additional sum for this. Specific accommodation has been listed by Area. In categorising the hotels, the editor has simplified the classification. *Super Deluxe* refers to *Gran turismo* hotels where prices are usually very expensive. *Moderate* refers to price in terms of European equivalents and not to the category of hotel which is

ACCOMMODATION/NIGHTLIFE AND ENTERTAINMENT

These brightly-coloured parrots found in Acapulco are typically Mexican

mainly 5- and 4-star.
Inexpensive includes 3- star
and 2-star hotels, and *Economy*
refers to 1-star hotels.
There are also hostels but
these are often run-down and
away from the centre of the
town and frequently no
cheaper than local hotels.

Helpful Hint

December is the high season.
Hotel rates are considerably
lower during the rest of the
year.
There is a variety of chain
hotels throughout the country.
Many international hotel chains
are represented and where
they are, accommodation may
be booked through their
offices abroad. These are the
major hotel groups with hotels
in Mexico:
Aston Hotels and Resorts, Best
Western International, Holiday
Inns International, Hyatt, Inter-
Continental, Marriot, Princess
Hotels International, Quality

Inns International (known as
Calinda Hotels in Mexico),
Kamada, Sheraton,
Utell/Stouffer Presidente, Villa
Vera, and Westin.

NIGHTLIFE AND ENTERTAINMENT

Mexico City has a rich cultural
life and its own world-famous
dance troupe, the **Ballet
Folklórico** which performs
regularly on Wednesdays
(21.00hrs) and Sundays (09.30
and 21.00hrs) at the **Palacio de
Bellas Artes** (National Institute
of Fine Arts) on Plaza Central
Alameda. Here you can also
attend operas and concerts.
The **National Auditorium**, in
Chapultepec Park, is a less
expensive venue, and concerts
are also held at two halls near
the Perisur shopping centre:
Ollin Yoliztli and
Nezahuacóyotil. Near Bellas
Artes is **El Teatro de la Ciudad
de México** (Theatre of the City

NIGHTLIFE AND ENTERTAINMENT/WEATHER

of Mexico).

Tickets for the theatre, cinema, sports and bull fights in Mexico City can be bought, with a 10 per cent surcharge, at the **Boletrónico** electronic service; but they must be bought at least 24 hours before the performance or event. Hotel desks have up-to-date information on the whereabouts of the service. Mexico's smaller towns will not usually provide a very lively nightlife, and visitors may find hotels their best bet for late-night entertainment and dancing. However, the major towns and cities have plenty of action; see the individual regions described earlier in the book for selected listings of discos and other nightlife.

WEATHER

Hollywood films have left the impression on many minds that Mexico is a hot arid land filled with desert, where only the cactus and a few hardy bandits can survive the climate. The temperature and rainfall depends mainly on altitude. Unlike people living in northern Europe, Mexicans do not have to go south for their sunshine, they have to descend.

The hot regions of Mexico, *tierras caldas*, are those below 10,000 feet (3,000m), such as the coast, the Yucatán, and the Balsas Valley. Here the average temperature is over 25°C (80°F) and in the summer often over 38°C (100°F). Such regions are the home of birds of colourful plumage and

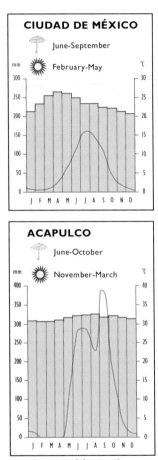

supply most of the exotic Mexican fruit, which visitors love to eat. Temperate regions, *tierras templades*, exist between 3,000 and 5,000 feet (914m and 1500m) and here is grown the robust maize which is the staple diet of so many Mexicans. In this region the average temperature is between 15° and 21°C (60° and 70°F).

Above this altitude lie the cold lands, *tierras frías*, or valleys enclosed by the cordilleras of the Sierra Madre Occidental and the Sierra Madre Oriental. In this region, with temperatures about 13°-18°C (55°-65°F), farmers grow wheat, maize and European species of fruits and vegetables. If visiting these areas it is advisable to have some warmer clothes as the daytime temperature can fall by 7.5°C (20°F) at night. However, not to totally disillusion keen film goers, it should be noted that Mexico does produce the greatest variety of cacti in the world. These grow in the arid deserts in the north of Mexico and the date palms of San Ignacio and Kada Kaurahang in Baja California match the finest groves in the Sahara. Incidentally, the name 'California' is derived from *calida fornax*, meaning 'hot oven'.

HOW TO BE A LOCAL

Mexico is a rich mix of races and cultures. Most of today's population is made up of *mestizos* – Spanish-Indians – but there are many 'pure' Indian communities. About 50 or so tribes form the core of the descendants of ancient Indian tribes, and many retain their old tribal lands, including communities such as the Tarahumaras, Mayas and Yaquis, and the Tzotzils and Tzeltals in the Chiapas highlands. Most of those descended from central Mexican tribes now live in villages around the Valley of Mexico. About three to four million people are officially said to be 'full blood' Indians, still speaking their native languages and holding on to their traditions. Although many of the Indians have taken up Christianity, not all have, and most combine the Christian tradition with their own religions and practises. Generally, visitors will find Mexicans friendly and polite but rather formal; you are not likely to blend in by being over-familiar.

Sexual roles are still quite strictly defined in Mexico; among the *mestizos* particularly, *machismo* exerts a strong influence and men can display an aggressive, swaggering image, while assuming a fiercely protective attitude to the women of their families. The maternal role is vitally important and mother–son bonds can be particularly strong. Foreign women, particularly from the West and travelling alone, should be prepared for the *macho* approach to women, which they may encounter in Mexico (see Personal Priorities below). The Indian population tends to display rather different characteristics, which can seem more passive. Although frequently very poor, 'pure' Indians have a most extraordinary dignity, which has perhaps been bequeathed to them from their ancient background. They, like other Mexicans, appreciate courtesy and respect from visitors.

PERSONAL PRIORITIES

There are plenty of pharmacies in Mexico (**see Directory**), and the general run of toiletries can be obtained from all but the smallest communities. But it is as well to bring certain items with you; aspirin, medication for minor injuries, insect repellent, contact lens solution, tampons and contraceptives, for example.

Do not carry drugs, as heavy fines and jail sentences can be imposed. If anyone approaches you trying to sell drugs, tell them to go away immediately: it could be a police trap. Nudity is against the law; be careful even when bathing in remote areas. Homosexuality is not against the law except between adults and minors.

Women travelling alone may well receive unwelcome attention. The best way to respond to comments or harassment is to ignore them; they are more often a nuisance than a threat.

Women should not go into *cantinas*, which are all-male.

SPECIAL EVENTS

Fiestas

Mexico has so many fiestas every year that it is only possible to list those which are celebrated nationwide.

1 January – New Year's Day. In the provinces many agricultural and livestock fairs take place around this date.

6 January – Feast of the Epiphany or Día de los Reyes (Day of the Kings), commemorates the bearing of gifts to the Infant Jesus. It is also the day that the 'Three Kings' bring gifts for Mexican children who set out their shoes hoping to have them filled.

17 January – Feast of Saint Anthony, The Blessing of the Animals. Household pets as well as cows, pigs and chickens are decked with flowers and ribbons and taken to church to be blessed.

2 February – Candlemas Day, or the Blessing of the Candles is the Feast of the Purification of the Virgin Mary. Impressive fiestas take place in Tlacotalpán and Veracruz.

5 February –Constitution Day. Celebrates the National Charter, which officially ended the Revolution of 1910.

February/March (date varies) in the week leading up to Lent which begins on Ash Wednesday – Mardi Gras festivities in the seaport cities.

March/April (date varies) Holy Week. Candlelit processions and Passion Plays.

April/May – Aquascalientes. Fería de San Marcos (San Marcos National Fair). Attractions include bullfights.

1 May – Labour Day. Parades, speeches. Everything closes.

3 May – Holy Cross Day. Celebrated by construction workers, who place crosses on top of unfinished buildings.

5 May – Anniversary of the Battle of Puebla (1862) in which Mexican troops defeated the Napoleonic invaders. Major celebrations nationwide.

10 May – Mother's Day. Special celebrations

throughout Mexico.

15 May – San Isidro Day.
Dedicated to the patron saint of farmers and agriculture.

1 June – Navy Day. Celebrated in major port cities with wreath-laying ceremonies.

May/June (60 days after Easter) Corpus Christi.
Religious ceremonies, and in Mexico City, children dressed in native costume are taken to the cathedral in the Zócalo for a blessing. In Papantla, Veracruz, the famous 'flying birdmen' perform their breathtaking dance, *El Volador*.

24 June – St John the Baptist.
Marked by religious services, processions and special fairs. In San Juan del Río, Querétaro the statue of the saint is taken to the river for its yearly bath.

16 July – Feast of Our Lady of Mount Carmel. Celebrated throughout Mexico with fireworks, games and bullfights. In San Angel, Mexico City there is a beautiful Flower Show.

25 July – Feast of Santiago (St James). Religious services and processions. Mexican-style rodeos are often held.

15 August – Feast of the Assumption of the Virgin Mary. Religious ceremonies and processions as well as the famous Bull Running in Huamantla.

1 September – State of the Union address given by the President. Banks and government offices close.

15-16 September – Independence Day. Starts on the night of 15th when, all over Mexico, public officials raise

Hidalgo's call *'Grito de Dolores'* that launched the War of Independence. In Mexico City, at 23.00hrs on 15th, the President of Mexico gives the shout from the balcony of the National Palace before a crowd of over half a million people gathered in the Zócalo. This is followed by a spectacular firework display. On 16th there is a military parade from the Zócalo to the Independence Monument.

4 October – Feast of St Francis of Assisi. Processions and parties. People called Francis or Frances receive gifts.

12 October – National Day or Columbus Day (Día de la Raza). Called Day of the Race because Columbus' discovery marked the beginning of a new race made up of Hispanics and indigenous people.

1 November – All Saints Day.
Religious ceremonies and processions.

2 November – All Souls Day (Día de la Muerta – The Day of the Dead). Candlelit all-night vigils are held at local cemeteries.

20 November – Anniversary of the Mexican Revolution of 1910. Parades throughout the country.

12 December – Feast of the Virgin of Guadalupe. The patron saint of Mexico is honoured.

16-25 December. The Christmas season features nightly *posadas* or processions with some people dressed as Joseph and Mary looking for room at an inn *(posada)*. Each night, the procession stops at a different house, asking to be let in to the building.

CHILDREN

A holiday in Mexico is great fun for children as there are so many marvellous beaches and special amusements for them. Mexico City, in particular, has an amusement park and zoo in **Chapultepec Park** and a marine park called **Atlantis**. Also in the park are several museums – Technology, Anthropology and Natural History. The **Ballet Folklórico** in the Palace of Fine Arts is particularly lively. Boat trips on the lagoons at the **Floating Gardens of Xochimilco** and the **Reino Aventura** (Adventure Park), **Zacango Zoo** and **Plaza Show**, with its prehistoric section and baby animals, are all within reach of Mexico City. Further afield are mining towns, caves and, of course pyramids and other ruins, as well as attractions like **Cici** marineland in Acapulco and amusement parks and zoos in Puebla, Monterrey, Guadalajara and Morelia. If you are travelling with children it is a good idea to take a selection of familiar medicines in a medical kit. Disposable nappies and ready prepared baby foods are available. Mexicans adore children and are very family-orientated. There are big transport and hotel price reductions for children and in many hotels they get free accommodation if they sleep in the parents' room. Many restaurants have special cheaper dishes for children. Tummy upsets are common, so consider carefully what you offer your children. Don't buy ice cream on the beach and avoid home-made sweets. There are hundreds of miles/kilometres of sandy beaches but there is often a strong undertow just off the shore. Pay attention to the colour of the flag that is flying on the beach and if in doubt use the swimming pool.

TIGHT BUDGET

The low cost of transport and cheap accommodation available combined with the weakness of the peso against other strong currencies makes living on a tight budget fairly easy. However, the developed resorts, big cities and along the border, are more expensive.

It is possible to eat cheaply in Mexico, but you may have to choose your establishment carefully. A snack bar or café is known as a *café, merendero, comedar* or *loncheria*. These cover a wide range of quality and cleanliness, though the food is never expensive. You can also eat in the market *fondas*, where the kitchen and the food are both on view and you can see what you are ordering. Bargaining is an accepted practice for shoppers – but should not be attempted in restaurants, government shops, hotel shops, or where the prices are fixed (*precios fijos*). Buses are efficient as well as cheap, the same applies to Mexico City's metro system. (See **Public Transport** in the **Directory** , and Mexico City, **Transport** page 40).

DIRECTORY

Arriving

Entry Formalities
Passports: Required by all except nationals of the USA and Canada holding proof of citizenship.
Tourist Card: Necessary for all visitors to Mexico. A Tourist Card ('FMT' in Spanish) is an entry–departure document (not a visa) which must be obtained before entry into Mexico. The card is issued free of charge by Mexican embassies (or consulates), tourist offices, travel agencies, or airlines serving Mexico. The areas of Mexico to be visited and the length of your stay (up to 90 days) must be specified. A Tourist Card is valid for **ONE** entry only, but is **NOT** required by American citizens who intend to spend no more than **three days** in Mexico, in border towns or ports.
Visas: A visa (replacing a Tourist Card) is required by nationals of Australia and New Zealand.

Under 18 years old
All persons under the age of 18 years if not travelling with **both** parents must contact the Mexican Embassy before departure.

By air
Airlines serving Mexico directly from the UK are American Airlines, Continental Airlines, British Airways/ Mexicana, Air France, Delta Airlines, Iberia, KLM, Lufthansa and Pan American. The approximate flight time from London to Mexico City is nine hours, including a stop over in the USA.
The independent traveller who may wish to stop over in the USA, either coming or going, will find that a wide range of scheduled airlines fly to destinations in North America from where he or she can pick up another flight, either by Mexicana Airlines or Aero México (the two national airlines), on to Mexico. Air fares are in a constant state of flux so it is worthwhile shopping around for the best bargain. Travel agents are a useful source of information on

DIRECTORY

these matters. Often small airlines such as Virgin Atlantic offer a particularly good deal. US Air, which has a large internal domestic service within the USA provides an excellent service for this type of stop-over.

Out of Britain there are now some 40 tour operators packaging holidays to Mexico. Among the leaders are such companies as Cathy Matos Mexican Tours, Falcon Holidays, Kuoni Travel, Speedbird Holidays, Swan Hellenic Art Treasure Tours, Thomas Cook, Thomson Worldwide, Tjareborg, Tradewinds and Faraway Holidays. Those providing their own charter flights include Worldwide Thomson, Kuoni, Pegasus and Falcon.

Mexico City *(Benito Juárez International)* is located 4½ miles (7km) east of the city (travel time 20 minutes). Buses to the city leave every 15 minutes between 06.00–22.00hrs. The return is from the Camino Real Hotel, Reforma Street (same hours). Courtesy coaches are laid on by some major hotels. The

Benito Juárez airport, Mexico City

metro station, *Terminal Aérea* (Line 5) – **NOT** *Aeropuerto* – is a 5-minute walk from the airport terminal, however there is a limited luggage allowance on the metro. For a taxi, go to desks marked *Venta de Boletos*; they will sell you a ticket which you present to any waiting car marked *Transporte Terrestre*.

Acapulco *(Internacional General Juan M Alvarez)* is situated 16 miles (26km) east of the city (travel time 30 minutes). Public bus to the city every 10 minutes (05.00–24.00hrs) and some hotel courtesy coaches. Taxis can be expensive; shared Chevrolet *combis* provide a better deal.

Guadalajara *(Internacional Miguel Hidalgo)* lies 12 miles (20km) south of the city (travel time 30 minutes). Bus to the city every 10 minutes (05.00–24.00hrs) plus courtesy coaches operated by some larger hotels.

Monterrey *(General Maríano Escobero)* lies 15 miles (24km) northeast of the city (travel times 45 minutes), bus and taxi services available.

Departure. Upon departure from the country, passengers have to pay airport tax which is, at the time of going to press, US$10 or the equivalent amount in pesos.

By Bus
North American services operated by Greyhound and Trailways run regularly to all major border crossings, and at the larger of these, their buses take passengers on to Mexican

bus stations. Both companies are able to reserve through-tickets with their Mexican counterparts. For services in Mexico see **Public Transport**.

By Rail
There is no direct rail connection between the USA and Mexico. You have to cross the border by some other form of transport, or on foot, to connect up with Mexican rail services (see **Public Transport** section).

By Road
The main points of entry from the USA into Mexico are:
Mexicali from San Diego;
Nogales from Phoenix/Tucson;
El Paso/Ciudad Juárez from Tucson and Alberquerque;
Eagle Pass/Piedras Negras from Del Río, San Angelo and El Paso;
Laredo/Nuevo Laredo from Houston, San Antonio and Del Río;
Brownsville/Matamoros from Houston and Galveston.
(See also **Driving**).

By Sea
A great number of cruise ships include Mexico in their itinerary. Many originate from across the Gulf at Miami and Fort Lauderdale, calling in at resorts such as Cancún and Cozumel in the Caribbean. Others originate from Los Angeles and San Diego and sail along the Pacific coastline calling in at Cabo San Lucas, Acapulco, Zihuatanejo, Ixtapa and Puerto Vallarta. Still others include both coasts and pass through the Panama Canal. Among the cruise lines which

call in at Mexico are Admiral Cruises, Cunard Crusader, Dolphin Cruise Line, Norwegian Caribbean, P & O Cruises, Princess Cruises, Royal Caribbean and the Royal Viking Line.

Camping
Mexico has very few organised campsites. Most are trailer parks situated just off major highways and not pleasant for pitching tents. You can camp anywhere in the national parks and no permits or fees are required; otherwise you can pitch your tent in any area away from main roads.

Chemist (see Pharmacist)

Crime
Despite soaring crime rates there is no undue danger, provided you stick to the beaten-track. Even in Mexico City, the scene of most serious crime, there is little more threat than the average inner city, though, as in all cities, there are areas best to avoid. Drug offences are the most common cause of **serious** trouble. A jail sentence can be expected for foreign visitors in the possession of even small quantities of drugs. For most tourists, however, the biggest worry is petty theft and pick-pockets. Money should never be too conspicuous; when travelling keep an eye on luggage.

Customs Regulations
Visitors over the age of 18 years can bring into Mexico the following goods duty-free:
400 cigarettes
or 2 boxes of cigars
or up to 250 grams of tobacco;

DIRECTORY

3 litres of spirits or wine; a reasonable quantity of perfume or eau-de-cologne; other goods up to the value of US$300, or equivalent; one photo, movie or video camera and up to 12 rolls of unexposed film or video cassettes.

Currency

You may bring into Mexico an unlimited amount of foreign currency, which must be declared to customs on arrival. You can not take out more than the declared amount.
Local currency up to 5,000 pesos may be imported or exported.

Disabled

Disabled travellers are likely to find that Mexico does not generally cater for their needs.

Driving

Bringing a car into Mexico requires motorists to be issued with a different kind of tourist card from other visitors (see **Arriving**) which ensures they cannot leave without their car. A Mexican car insurance policy, which is expensive, is also required – it is available from agencies on both sides of the border but probably more easily negotiated in the USA. Most foreign licences are valid in Mexico but European ones may be unfamiliar so it is a good idea to carry an International Driving Permit (available from the AA in Britain – it is different from the one which covers driving in the USA).
Many visitors from overseas like to fly and drive or hire a car while on holiday. This can be arranged as many of the international car-hire firms have offices at airports, city centres and in resorts. There are many local operations, too, but make very sure you are well insured against accidents. There are cars in Mexico that would never pass their roadworthy tests back home.

Breakdown

To help motorists, Mexico has an effective 'Green Angel' *(Angeles Verde)* service, a fleet of white and green, radio-dispatched emergency vehicles which patrol the roads and highways. Labour is provided free, although a tip is appreciated. Spare parts are charged at cost. If you need assistance and are not 'spotted' call the Green Angels on 250–8221.
Warning
If you see an accident you should **not** go to help, but notify the first policeman or 'Green Angel' patrolman that you can find. If you move an injured person you can be accused of *mal medicinia* and if the person dies, you can even be accused of causing the death.

Parking

Parking is not easy in cities and if you wish to avoid being towed away, use an *estacionamiento* (parking lot).

Roads

Mexico's highway system is well-developed with tolls payable for use of motorways. Away from the large centres of population roads are quite often narrow, winding and pot-holed. Also look out for *topes* (sleeping policemen) across the road, before and after most villages.

Electricity

The supply is 110 volts AC, 60 Hz, though fluctuations in the current can occur. Sockets accept simple two (flat) pin plugs. Most North American electrical appliances can be used, but appliances from Britain, Australia or New Zealand will need a voltage transformer, unless fitted with a dual-voltage switch. A plug adaptor is also necessary.

Embassies and Consulates

The main embassies are all in Mexico City but several countries have consular representatives in other large towns.
UK—Río Lerma 71, Colon Cuauhtémoc, 06500 Mexico City 5, DF (tel: (5) 514-33-27 and (5) 514-38-86).
Consulado (Consulate): Río Usumacinta 30, Colon Cuauhtémoc, 06500 Mexico City, DF (tel: (5) 511-48-80).
Australia—Jaime Balmes 11-B-1002, Colon Los Morales, 11510 Mexico City, DF (tel: (5) 395-98-69 and (5) 395-96-69).
Canada—Schiller 529, Colon Polanco, 11560 Mexico City, DF (tel: (5) 254-32-88).
USA—Ave Paseo de la Reforma 305, Colon Cuauhtémoc, 06500 Mexico City, DF (tel: (5) 211-00-42).
Eire (consulate)—Chapultepec 18, Mexico City, DF (tel: (5) 510-38-67).
New Zealand—Homero 229, Mexico City, DF (tel: (5) 566-10-10).

Emergency Phone Numbers

Federal Police (*Highway Patrol*)	684-2142
Fire	768-3700
Green Angels (*Angeles Verde*) Tourist Patrol	250-8221
Government Police	06
Mexico City Emergency Number	07
Red Cross (*Cruz Roja*) Ambulance	(5) 557-5758 or 557-4294
Secretaria de Turismo (Ministry of Tourism) (24-hour emergency hotline)	(5) 250 0123

Entertainment Information

Local tourist offices (*Turismo*) give details of what is going on in their area. The English-language newspaper, *Mexico City News* has a useful listings section. A weekly publication published on Friday called *Tiempo Libre* also gives information about events.

Health Regulations

There are, at present, no inoculations required to enter Mexico, unless you have visited a cholera infected area within the two weeks prior to your entry to Mexico, in which case a cholera vaccination certificate is demanded.
The greatest threat to health in Mexico is water – it should be boiled or sterilised. Milk should be boiled.
Some form of health insurance is essential. Public health care can be fairly rudimentary but on the whole, medical facilities in privately-run hospitals and clinics are good. Your hotel or embassy should be able to refer you to an English-speaking doctor or dentist.

Holidays

The main public holidays when virtually everything closes are:

1 January	New Year's Day
6 January	Epiphany
5 February	Constitution Day
21 March	Benito Juárez Day
March/April	Easter – Maundy Thursday, Good Friday and Easter Sunday
1 May	Labour Day
5 May	Battle of Puebla
15/16 September	Independence Day
12 October	National Day
20 November	Anniversary of the Revolution
12 December	Festival of the Virgin of Guadalupe
25 December	Christmas Day

In addition, every town or village will take at least one day off a year for a Fiesta – (see also section – **Fiestas**). Details from the nearest tourist office *(turismo)*.

Lost Property

Report it to the local police headquarters if you can make yourself understood, or if it is something more serious, a lost passport, for instance, report it to your embassy or consulate.

Media

Press

The daily English-language newspaper, the *Mexico City News*, is available in Mexico City and larger towns and resorts. There are also free English-language news-spreads such as the *Daily Bulletin* which can be picked up in Mexico City or tourist centres – either in large hotels or from tourist offices. American, British and other foreign newspapers are available from large hotels and bookshops, such as *Sanborn's*, though a few days late.

Radio

Mexico City's *Radio XEVIP* (AM 1560) broadcasts news and programmes in English throughout the day. Stations in other cities have several hours of English-language programmes each day. In some parts of the country, American radio broadcasts can be picked up, while the *BBC World Service* is also received, the best reception on 11.75 MHz, in the evening.

Money Matters

Mexico's unit of currency is the **peso**, comprising 100 **centavos**. Coins are in denominations of 20 and 50 centavos, and 1, 5, 10, 20, 50, 100 and 200 pesos. Notes come in 500, 1,000, 2,000, 5,000, 10,000 and 20,000 pesos. The peso is written as $. So as not to confuse it with the American dollar ($US) it is sometimes written as $MN (for *Moneda Nacional*). Currency rates can fluctuate daily due to the **peso's** weakness against other strong currencies. Banks generally give the best rate but exchange houses *(Casas de Cambio)* offer competitive rates (see **Opening Times** for business hours). Avoid changing large amounts in hotels and always check rates as some hotel exchange fees

Fiesta is the spirit of Mexico

are as high as 15 per cent. American dollars can be changed throughout the country but other currencies may be much harder to change outside the big cities. Credit cards and travellers cheques in US dollar denominations are most readily accepted. Most international credit cards are widely accepted in the larger cities and resorts.

Many hotels, restaurants and some stores and markets accept US dollars (usually at a worse rate); it is a good idea to carry a small calculator as well as some local currency.

Opening Times

It is almost impossible to generalise about opening times in Mexico – even when times are posted in museums, shops, etc, they are not strictly adhered to. The *siesta* is still widely in evidence, usually from 13.00 to 15.00hrs but for up to four hours along the hotter Gulf Coast and in the Yucatán. In the north and highland areas hours are more standard and there is sometimes no siesta.

Times below present a general picture:

Offices	08.00–15.00hrs Monday to Friday.
Shops:	*(Mexico City)* 09.00–20.00hrs Monday to Saturday *(Elsewhere)* 09.00–14.00hrs and 16.00–20.00hrs Monday to Friday.
Banks:	09.00–13.30hrs Monday to Friday. (Exchange houses – *Casas de Cambio* are open until later.)
Post Offices:	08.00–18.00hrs Monday to Friday (in large cities).
Museums/ Galleries:	Generally 09.00–13.00hrs and 15.00–18.00hrs, but closed Sunday afternoons and all day Monday.
Archaeological Sites:	Open all day.

Personal Safety

Despite alarmist reports about *banditos*, Mexico is a surprisingly safe place to travel. You should, however, not act in such a way as to draw attention to yourself and in any confrontation back off. Large cities demand extra attention, but provided you stick to busy, well-lit streets, and avoid lonely train stations, underpasses and public parks after dark, you should be safe (see also **Crime**).

A bigger threat to personal safety is perhaps through a natural event – the threat of a future disastrous earthquake is forever there, especially in Mexico City!

Pharmacist

Look for a green cross and the word *farmacia*. Pharmacists can be very useful, most speak English and are able to diagnose and treat minor ailments. Many drugs are often available without the prescription necessary in Britain or the USA, but be warned, some drugs are on sale which have been banned elsewhere.

The most common ailment of visitors to Mexico is diarrhoea, known as *turista* – most pharmacists are well used to this problem and the single word *diarrea* is often enough to be given the appropriate medicine.

In every town at least one *farmacia* remains open 24 hours, known as the *farmacia de la guardia* – hotel receptionists or tourist offices should be able to tell you which one.

Places of Worship

Mexico is a Catholic country (93 per cent) and, no matter how small a village is, there is bound to be a church there. The Catholic services are in Spanish, but it is possible to find services in English in Mexico City, Guadalajara, Cuernavaca, Acapulco and Monterrey. Until relatively recently women needed to cover their heads when entering churches; this is not always the case today.

Your hotel, the local tourist office or your consulate will be able to supply you with addresses and times of services, and English services are listed in *The News* every Friday. The following is a selection of places of worship with English-language services.

Acapulco

Catholic:	Maranatha Church, Calle Juan Sebastian.
Episcopal:	Holy Cross Episcopal Church, behind Hotel Las Vegas.
Interdenominational:	Chapel of Peace, Las Brisas.
Jewish:	Shalom Restaurant, Posada del Sol.

Cuernavaca:

Catholic:	Third Order Catholic Church on cathedral grounds.
Episcopal:	St Michael and All Angels Episcopal Church, Guerrero at Degollado.

Guadalajara

Baptist:	Gethsemane Baptist Church, Colomos 2148.

| Catholic: | Our Lady of Guadalupe, Tepeyac; and Fr Juan de Zumamaga, Colonia Chapalita. |
| Episcopal: | St Mark's, Azteca and Chichimecas, in Colonia Lomas del Valle. |

Mexico City

Baptist:	Capital City Baptist Church, Bondojito and Calle Sur 138.
Catholic:	St Patrick's, Bondojito 248; and Our Lady of Lourdes, Castillo de Chapultepec 70, Lomas de Chapultepec.
Episcopal:	Christ Church Episcopal, Calle Sierra Madre 210, Colonia las Lomas.
Jewish:	Beth Israel Community Centre, Virreyes 1140; Nidjei Israel Synagogue, Calle Acapulco 70; Mount Sinai Temple, Querétaro 110.

Monterrey

| Episcopal: | Holy Family, Somberete and Teotihuacán. |
| Interdenomi-national: | Union Church of Monterrey, Oscar Castillon 200. |

Police

The District Police Force maintains public order and safety and is in charge of traffic control. The police have certain duties relating specifically to visitors and their protection: to prevent private citizens from acting as unauthorized guides; to prevent the detention of foreign citizens or vehicles over small violations (though you should not take this as an excuse to violate the laws); to look out for merchants who raise their prices; and to give information and directions.

If you park illegally, your licence plates may be taken away. If this happens, or if you commit a minor traffic violation, you may be able to rectify the situation by offering the policeman a 'fine'; these *mordidas* (little bites) are quite common and may be suggested by the officer.

A special 'Language Police Force' is planned in Mexico City for the benefit of English-speaking visitors, to be based between the Museum of Anthropology and the National History Centre.

Post Office

Mexican postal services *(correos)* can be very slow, though fairly dependable. Airmail to the USA takes around a week, and two weeks to Europe and other destinations. If mail is important take it to the post office rather than drop it in a post box. You can also buy stamps and post mail through your hotel desk.

DIRECTORY

Public Transport

Air

Travel within Mexico is inexpensive and some thirty main airports throughout the country are serviced by the two major domestic lines, *Mexicana* and *Aeroméxico*. Other domestic airlines also provide a service. At one time there could be long delays at airports waiting for flights but this situation has improved a lot recently. There is not always a direct service from one main airport to another and it may often be necessary to fly back to Mexico City and change instead of flying on directly to a desired destination.

Most flights are between Mexico City and Guadalajara (more than ten a day) taking 55 minutes. There is a departure tax on internal flights, currently 3,500 pesos.

Rail

Starting with main stations, Tijuana and Mexicali in the north, the networks service important central and coastal cities and venture as far south as Mérida in the east and Tapachula in the west. The comfort of rail travel in Mexico is to a great extent governed by cost. Second class *(segunda clase)* travel is cheap but the seats are poorly padded and the carriages inclined to be crowded and hot or cold according to the weather outside. The scene may be picturesque but uncomfortable. Regular first class *(primera general clase)* carriages are usually air conditioned, comfortable and less crowded. In first class, *Primera Reservada* (or *Especial*), you get a reserved seat (usually reclining), in an air-conditioned and roomy carriage. For sleepers you pay a supplement over the top first class rate. The least expensive are curtained off bunks *(camas)*, in Pullman-style carriages.

It is advisable to book fares in advance. On the day, in smaller stations, tickets are not often sold until the train arrives in the station which frequently causes jostling and hustling. If you board without a ticket, the collector will charge and extra 25 per cent on the fare. If tickets are sold out, it is possible, on occasions, to buy direct from the porter for a few extra dollars.

Buses

The most common and efficient form of public transport. Seven hundred bus lines operate in Mexico itself, and despite the size of the country there is hardly a place that cannot be reached by bus. Fares are very cheap and there is a first *(primera)* and second *(segunda)* class service. Few second class vehicles are new. They are eventually relegated to junkyards but that can take quite a long time, so they can be fairly uncomfortable. First class tickets assign seats and some second class new buses, which operate long haul routes, do the same. Generally speaking, second class services are far more crowded, less comfortable and

There are four types of taxi in Mexico City – colour coded!

noisier than first class. On your first class ticket is marked the number of the bus *(camión)*, the hour of departure and the destination. Upon purchase, make sure you check that the details on your ticket are correct.

Luggage can be checked through to your final destination and you need to retain your check stub for collection.

Urban Services

In Mexico City there is an excellent and cheap metro system, with frequent trains and a flat fare. There is also a small tramway network and extensive bus and trolley-bus services. The latter has recently been modernised and operates a flat fare system. (See also **Mexico City – Transport**).

Guadalajara has a state-run bus and underground trolley service, also extensive private buses.

Taxis

Four different types operate in Mexico City:

— metered yellow-and-white taxis (usually Volkswagens) which must be hailed;
— *sitio*, orange-coloured and available at taxi-stands, also metered but it is best to agree a fare first;
— *turismo* (tourist) taxis with English-speaking drivers, not metered and a fare should be agreed before starting a journey;
— *pesero*, green-and-white, shared taxis travelling on fixed routes with fares charged according to distance travelled.

Senior Citizen Travel

Benefits to senior citizens (over 60) similar to students are also available. Write to Instituto Nacional de Lasenectuo, Concepcion Beistegui 13, Col

Deivaille 03100, Mexico DF (tel: (5) 536-24-88 and (5) 536-24-59).

Student Travel

There are considerable benefits connected with travelling and visiting places of interest, available to students with the right documentation, and those planning their holiday in advance and wishing to take advantage of these opportunities should write to CREA, Serapío Rendon 76, Colonía San Rafael, Mexico 06470 DF (tel: (5) 546-85-05 and (5) 591-01-44).

Telephones

Long-distance and international calls from Mexico are very expensive and it is advisable to place reversed charge calls *(por cobrar)* when calling home. This works out at half the price, or less, of direct-dial calls, though you can be charged whether you get through or not.

Calls out of Mexico can be placed anywhere displaying the blue-and-white *Larga Distancia* sign. Most *Telefonos* offices also offer the service. Unless you wish to make a direct-dial call, the procedure is that you dial 09 for the English-speaking international operator who connects you and presents you with a bill afterwards (you can keep an eye on the cost which clicks up on a meter). You can also make calls from hotels but they always carry an add-on price, so check first.

Local calls in Mexico on the other hand are ridiculously cheap. In Mexico City, local calls from old phone boxes are usually free, while new ones take coins of one peso or more. To make long-distance calls within Mexico dial 92, plus the telephone code and number (station to station), or 92 plus the telephone code and number (person to person). For the national operator call 02; for information dial 04.

To call Mexico from abroad dial the international access code (010 from Britain), plus the code for Mexico (52), followed by the area code, then the number.

Calling home is very expensive!

Time

Mexico spans three time zones. Expressed in relation to Greenwich Mean Time (GMT) these are:

General Mexico Time (GMT minus 6)

— General, Coahuila,
  Durango, Nuevo León, and
  Tamaulipas.
Mountain Time (GMT minus 7)
— Nayarit, Sinaloa, Sonora,
  and Baja California Sur.
Pacific Time (GMT minus 8)
— Baja California Norte.

Daylight Saving

Comes into operation in some
parts of Mexico during the
summer, when clocks are put
forward an hour. This affects
the areas: Coahuila, Durango,
Nuevo León, and Tamaulipas
where local time becomes
GMT minus 5, while time in
Baja California Norte becomes
GMT minus 7.

Tipping

Service charges are rarely
added to hotel, restaurant or
waiter-service bar bills, a tip
should be given in these
circumstances. Waiters expect
10–20 per cent of the bill if no
service charge has been
added. Porters get at least 200
pesos per bag. Taxi drivers do
not expect tips unless you have
small change left over or you
hire them for several hours.
Ushers and washroom
attendants receive small
gratuities.

Toilets

Public toilets are known
usually as *baños* (literally
'bathrooms') or as *excusados,
sanitarios* or *servicios*. They
are mostly unhygienic affairs,
with a shortage of paper
(though it may be sold outside).
Most often you will see the
signs *Damas* (Ladies) and
Caballeros (Gentlemen),
otherwise you will come across

the potentially confusing
Señoras (Women) and *Señores*
(Men).

Tourist Offices

The *Secretaria de Turismo
(SecTur)* has offices *(Turismo)*
in Mexico City and throughout
the country. Their main office
is at: Presidente Masaryk 172,
11587 Mexico City (tel. (5)
250-8555).
There is a 24-hour tourist
information 'hotline': (5)
250-1023.
In addition there are tourist
offices run by state and
municipal authorities and often
you will find several rival
operations in the same town.
The local telephone directory
gives the address and phone
number of both federal and
local tourist offices.

LANGUAGE

Pronunciation

Vowels All Spanish vowel
sounds are pure. The final **e** is
always pronounced.

Pronounce **a** as in (father)
         e as in (bed)
         ai as in (air)
         i as in (machine)
         o as in (low)
         u as in (ruin)

Consonants

Similar to English consonants
with some exceptions, ie:
Pronounce
         n as in (canyon)
         ll as a 'y'
           (yoghurt)
         g as 'h' except
           when followed
           by 'u'
         h is silent
         qu as 'k' (cane)

LANGUAGE

Words which end in a vowel, **n** or **s** are stressed on the last syllable but one, eg **ca**sa, **ga**fas, **ven**den. Words which end in a consonant other than **n** or **s** are stressed on the last syllable, eg ha**blar**, espa**nol**. A written accent mark will indicate exceptions to this rule, eg café, autobús, estación.

Numbers

1	uno
2	dos
3	tres
4	cuatro
5	cinco
6	seis
7	siete
8	ocho
9	nueve
10	diez
11	once
12	doce
13	trece
14	catorce
15	quince
16	diez y seis
17	diez y siete
18	diez y ocho
19	diez y nueve
20	veinte
21	veinte y uno
22	veinte y dos
23	veinte y tres
24	veinte y cuatro
30	treinta
40	cuarenta
50	cincuenta
60	sesenta
70	setenta
80	ochenta
90	noventa
100	cien (or) ciento
1000	mil

Days of the Week

Monday	Lunes
Tuesday	Martes
Wednesday	Miércoles
Thursday	Jueves
Friday	Viernes
Saturday	Sábado
Sunday	Domingo

Months (*meses*)

January	Enero
February	Febrero
March	Marzo
April	Abril
May	Mayo
June	Junio
July	Julio
August	Agosto
September	Septiembre
October	Octubre
November	Noviembre
December	Diciembre

Basic Phrases

Good morning/good day Buenos días
Good afternoon Buenas tardes
Good evening/good night Buenas noches
Good-bye Adiós
Hello Hola
How are you? Cómo está usted?
Very well, thank you Muy bien, gracias
See you soon Hasta luego
Have a good journey Buen viaje!
Good luck/all the best Buena suerte!
Sorry/excuse me Perdone
That's all right Está bien
Everything all right? De nada?
Don't worry No se preocupe
It doesn't matter No importa
I beg your pardon? Qué/cómo dice?
Am I disturbing you? (Le) molesto?
I'm sorry to have troubled you Siento haberle molestado
Good/that's fine Bien/está muy bien

INDEX/ACKNOWLEDGEMENTS

The Automobile Association would like to thank the following photographers and libraries for their assistance in the preparation of this book:

PETER WILSON took all the photographs (© AA Photolibrary) except:

MARY EVANS PICTURE LIBRARY 21 Spaniards destroy Aztec sculptures, 22 Cortés advances

NATURE PHOTOGRAPHERS LTD 89 Rainforest (N P Williams), 91 Cardon cactus (P R Sterry), 92 Flycatcher, 93 Large forest butterfly (N P Williams), 94 Great blue heron (P R Sterry), 95 Green lizard, 97 Usumacinta Marshes (N P Williams), 99 Gray whale, 100 Los Islotes (P R Sterry)

SPECTRUM COLOUR LIBRARY Cover: Fisherman, 34 Museum of Anthropology

ZEFA PICTURE LIBRARY (UK) LTD 119 Fiesta

MEXICAN TOURIST BOARD 6/7 Island of Janítzio, 8 Baja California